DOCTOR FAUSTUS

CHRISTOPHER MARLOWE

Oxford
Literature
Companions

Notes and activities: Graham Elsdon
Series consultant: Peter Buckroyd

OXFORD
UNIVERSITY PRESS

Contents

Introduction

What are Oxford Literature Companions?

Oxford Literature Companions is a series designed to provide you with comprehensive support for popular set texts. You can use the Companion alongside your play, using relevant sections during your studies or using the book as a whole for revision.

Each Companion includes detailed guidance and practical activities on:

- **Plot and Structure**
- **Context**
- **Genre**
- **Characterisation and Roles**
- **Language**
- **Themes**
- **Performance**
- **Critical Views**
- **Skills and Practice**

How does this book help with exam preparation?

As well as providing guidance on key areas of the play, throughout this book you will also find 'Upgrade' features. These are tips to help with your exam preparation and performance.

In addition, in the extensive **Skills and Practice** chapter, the 'Exam skills' section provides detailed guidance on areas such as how to prepare for the exam, understanding the question, planning your response and hints for what to do (or not do) in the exam.

In the **Skills and Practice** chapter there is also a bank of **Sample questions** and **Sample answers**. The **Sample answers** are marked and include annotations and a summative comment.

How does this book help with terminology?

Throughout the book, key terms are highlighted in the text and explained on the same page. There is also a detailed **Glossary** at the end of the book that explains, in the context of the play, all the relevant literary terms highlighted in this book.

Which edition of the play has this book used?

Quotations and character names have been taken from Oxford Student Texts edition of *Doctor Faustus* (ISBN 978-019-832599-4). Please note: this edition of the play follows the A text.

How does this book work?

Each book in the Oxford Literature Companions series follows the same approach and includes the following features:

- **Key quotations** from the play
- **Key terms** explained on the page and linked to a complete glossary at the end of the book
- **Activity boxes** to help improve your understanding of the text
- **Upgrade** tips to help prepare you for your assessment

Upgrade tips to help prepare you for your assessment

Activity boxes to help improve your understanding of the play

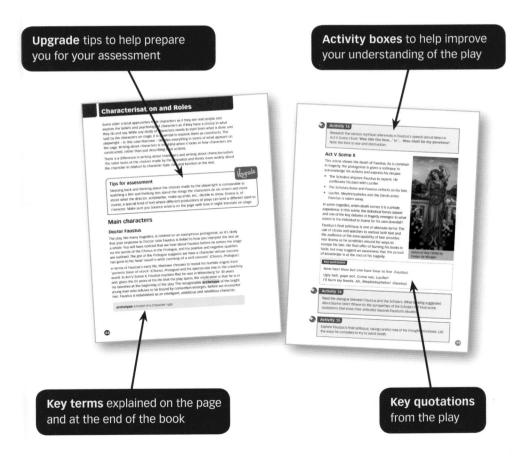

Key terms explained on the page and at the end of the book

Key quotations from the play

Versions of the play

Doctor Faustus is a brilliant, multifaceted play whose appeal to 21st-century audiences lies partly in its variety. The story places tragedy alongside **farce** in a way that some modern drama does: it refuses to be easily categorised. Its resistance to simple definition is part of its attraction, yet the lack of a definitive text version of the play also poses an issue for students.

Of the two versions of the play in publication, the A text (from 1604) is shorter, whereas the longer B text (from 1616) contains material that may have been written by other playwrights. The following plot summaries are based on the A text version published by OUP and edited by Richard Gill. As part of your studies, you should make yourself aware of the differences in content between the two versions.

Unlike a prose novel, where a narrator offers you a way to understand characters and events, drama relies on performance to reveal feelings and motivation. Drama shows, rather than tells. As you study *Doctor Faustus*, take note of the way the drama is structured. Consider when characters enter and exit the stage, who speaks, who is silent and what the audience – and the characters – do *and* don't know at various points.

Although you will probably be reading *Doctor Faustus* 'on the page', try to view a performance on stage or on film in order to appreciate fully the dramatic effect of the play. The recording of the 2011 Shakespeare's Globe production is particularly good in this respect. You should be aware that different directors will choose to perform the play in different ways, subtly altering the way lines are delivered, facial expression, movement, costume, setting, staging and timing.

Plot

Prologue

The play begins with a speech by the **Chorus**, whose words give the audience Faustus's **backstory**, telling of his early life and achievements. The Prologue also gives an outline of the **character arc** of the **protagonist** in the play, so the audience knows, even before Faustus enters on stage, that he will make a fatal choice and by implication lose his life.

We learn that Faustus:

- was from a humble background
- became a doctor of divinity (theology)
- had ambitions that led him to engage in necromancy (dark magic)
- turned away from God and suffered for it.

In starting the play with what is effectively a spoiler, you may think that any dramatic tension about Faustus's fate is removed. This may be true, but the effect is one of **dramatic irony**. In knowing the outcome of events, the audience watch the play differently – the focus is placed on the journey towards the protagonist's inevitable disaster. With each warning he rejects and each choice he makes, the audience see the stages in his downfall.

You will notice that the language used by the Chorus is heroic and elevated in nature. References to Mars (the Roman god of war) and the battlefield where Hannibal defeated the Romans give a sense of grandeur. This also creates a sense of irony, as Faustus's story is anything but a heroic tale – it's a story of evil choices and destruction. The reference to the story of Icarus provides a telling parallel to Faustus's overreaching and disregard for good advice.

backstory events that have happened before the play begins

character arc the 'journey' of a character during a story

Chorus a character(s) who offers comment on the action of the play to the audience

dramatic irony where the audience possess more knowledge than the character(s) on stage

farce a comic dramatic work including crude characterisation and ridiculously improbable situations

protagonist the central character; sometimes, but not always, a hero

The story of Icarus

The story of Icarus comes from Greek myth. In *Metamorphoses*, Ovid relays the tale of Icarus and his father Daedalus, who are trying to escape Crete. Daedalus makes some wings from feathers and wax. Despite warnings about not flying too close to the sun, Icarus ignores the advice and the sun melts the wax, which causes Icarus to plummet into the sea, where he perishes.

The Fall of Icarus (1636) by Peter Paul Rubens

Key quotations

… born, his parents base of stock *(Chorus)*

His waxen wings did mount above his reach *(Chorus)*

Nothing so sweet as magic is to him *(Chorus)*

Activity 1

One of the choices Marlowe makes is to tell the audience of Faustus's humble background. Why might Marlowe have included this information?

Act I Scene I

This scene is set in Faustus's study. In performance, the set often has rows of bookcases and a desk to signify the Doctor's academic life. The function of the scene is to establish aspects of Faustus's personality and show why and how he becomes embroiled in necromancy (dark magic).

- Faustus debates the limits of disciplines such as logic, domestic economy, medicine and divinity.
- He extols the virtues and power of necromancy.
- The Good Angel and the Evil Angel offer their advice.
- Valdes and Cornelius, two magicians, encourage Faustus and agree to teach him magic.
- Faustus decides to learn necromancy even though it will destroy him.

In many ways, Faustus appears arrogant and unfulfilled despite his achievements. His decision to follow the dark path is based on a desire for power and knowledge. The Good and Evil Angels offer advice and may be seen as dramatic representations of the internal conflict Faustus feels. You will notice that he doesn't interact with these characters.

Valdes and Cornelius (who together with Faustus might be seen as an ironic parallel of the Holy Trinity) offer Faustus a glimpse of the power he can possess. As you read the play, take note of how he uses this power and whether it lives up to the image that Valdes and Cornelius offer him.

Activity 2

Make notes on each of the areas listed below. Choose a quotation that summarises each one.

- Why Faustus is frustrated by the various branches of learning
- What Faustus says he will do with his new powers
- The powers and experiences Valdes and Cornelius suggest Faustus will have

Act I Scene II

An element of comedy is present in this scene between Wagner, Faustus's servant, and the two Scholars. In performance, the Scholars are often presented as austere figures whose scholarly demeanour contrasts with that of the dangerously exciting Valdes and Cornelius.

- The two Scholars arrive, wishing to see Faustus.
- Wagner teases them and then reveals where Faustus is.
- The Scholars express their horror at the prospect of Faustus practising magic.

The humour comes in part from the language used by Wagner, which mimics the logical arguments of Faustus and sounds comical from the mouth of a servant. It acts as a **parody** of the argument Faustus expounds in the previous scene. A further layer of irony is present in the fact that Wagner outwits his supposedly more intellectual superiors. Aside from the comic material, the Scholars offer a reminder of the way Faustus's fatal choice would be viewed by many people.

> **parody** imitation of a person or thing for comic effect

Activity 3

Write a paragraph exploring why Marlowe might wish to undermine the Scholars comically and why a director might choose to present them as unexciting and slow-witted.

Act I Scene III

This is a key scene in the early phase of the play, containing the first appearance of Mephistopheles (a servant of Lucifer) and Faustus's proposal to give over his soul. Dramatically, the scene is quite intense.

Christians believe that God consists of three aspects: the Father, the Son and the Holy Spirit.

Key quotations

The reward of sin is death. That's hard. *(Faustus)*

... necromantic books are heavenly. *(Faustus)*

A sound magician is a mighty god. *(Faustus)*

This night I'll conjure, though I die therefore. *(Faustus)*

The Latin spell, elements of dark magic and the imposing entrance of Mephistopheles create a darkly supernatural feel.

- Faustus conducts his spell to conjure Mephistopheles.
- Mephistopheles enters. Faustus instructs him to return dressed as a Franciscan friar.
- Mephistopheles explains about Lucifer to Faustus and warns him to turn away from necromancy.
- Faustus offers his soul to Lucifer in exchange for 24 years of voluptuousness (behaviour that will bring pleasure).
- Mephistopheles agrees to consult Lucifer and return with an answer.
- Faustus appears to be enthralled by Mephistopheles.

Rather than being a simple tempter of Faustus, Marlowe decides to make Mephistopheles a more interesting character by having him express his own torment and also offer a further warning to Faustus.

Key quotations

Why, this is hell, nor am I out of it. *(Mephistopheles)*

Had I as many souls as there be stars, I'd give them all for Mephistopheles. *(Faustus)*

Michael Feast as Mephistopheles in the English Renaissance Drama production, 2004

Act I Scene IV

Once again, a comic scene follows one of high drama, with the action offering an ironic parallel to the Faustus scenes. Notice how Wagner's attempt to engage a servant mirrors his master's.

- Wagner tries to persuade Robin to act as his servant by offering money and threats.
- When Robin refuses, Wagner raises Balioll and Belcher, two devils, after which Robin agrees to Wagner's request.

The implication is that Wagner has been learning magic from Faustus's books, but there is no suggestion that Wagner has had to sell his soul, which raises a question about why Faustus has done so. Some of the language also contains ironic reference to Faustus's actions, with Wagner commenting that Robin would 'give his soul to the devil for a shoulder of mutton'.

Act II Scene I

The opening of the second act is one of dramatic spectacle, containing the pact of blood that Faustus makes with Lucifer, the mysterious words appearing on his arm and dancing devils. In terms of the story, it is another key moment in which Faustus completes his fatal decision, despite some wavering.

- In his study, Faustus wonders in his **soliloquy** whether it is too late to repent.
- The Good and Evil Angels enter, offering contrasting advice.
- Mephistopheles enters, explaining that Lucifer requires a gift of blood to formalise the deal.
- Faustus cuts his arms but the blood congeals. Mephistopheles then offers fire to liquefy the blood.
- A warning appears written on Faustus's arm – *'Homo, fuge!'* (Flee, O Man).
- Mephistopheles arranges dancing devils with rich apparel to appear.
- Faustus gives a scroll to Mephistopheles containing his contract.
- Faustus and Mephistopheles discuss hell.
- Faustus demands a wife. An undesirable female devil appears and Mephistopheles tells him that he will bring courtesans (prostitutes) to Faustus.
- Mephistopheles gives Faustus a book containing powerful spells.

Activity 4

Read the **dialogue** between Faustus and Mephistopheles beginning at **'Now, Faustus, what wouldst thou...'** Make a list of quotations to express Mephistopheles's explanation of:

- his relationship with Lucifer
- why he appeared to Faustus
- how they came to be in hell with Lucifer
- the nature of his torment
- his advice to Faustus.

You could use a table like this:

Location	Explanation of...	Quotation
Act I, Scene III	His relationship with Lucifer	**I am a servant to great Lucifer**

dialogue an exchange of lines between two or more characters

soliloquy a speech made by an actor alone on stage, generally reflecting on thoughts and feelings

The central idea in this scene is that of a man who overlooks the warning signs. The advice of the Good Angel, an externalisation of Faustus's doubts, is ignored. The congealed blood and written message are presumably some supernatural warning too. Faustus fails to recognise Mephistopheles's distracting techniques and overlooks the fact that his first real request – a wife – cannot be provided.

Activity 5

a) Look carefully at Mephistopheles's **asides 'O, what will not I do...'** and **'I'll fetch him...'** What do they reveal about his attitude towards Faustus?

b) Explore the dialogue about hell from **'Now, Faustus, ask...'** to **'Walking, disputing, etc.?'** Compare Faustus's and Mephistopheles's perceptions of this place.

Key quotations

To him I'll build an altar and a church,
And offer lukewarm blood of new-born babes. *(Faustus)*

My blood congeals, and I can write no more. *(Faustus)*

I think hell's a fable. *(Faustus)*

Act II Scene II

This brief comic scene shows how Robin has acquired one of Faustus's books and intends to use magic for his own ends.

- Robin enters, reading a magic book, claiming he will now be able to make local maidens dance naked for him.
- He decides to use magic to get free drinks at the local inn.
- He assures Rafe that he will now be able to command the attention of Nan Spit.

Once again, a comic episode mimics Faustus's actions. You will have noticed that supposed magic is being put to superficial uses. It is debatable whether Faustus himself ever uses his magic for anything useful during the course of the play, so Marlowe's placement of this comic scene offers an ironic parallel to the protagonist's actions.

Act II Scene III

This is another scene that shows Faustus wavering only to be persuaded to stick with devilry. Once again, the scene is a lavish spectacle. We join the action in what seems to be the middle of a dialogue in which Faustus curses Mephistopheles and the Good and Evil Angels offer encouragement. After some dispute, Lucifer and Beelzebub appear and offer the dramatic representation of the Seven Deadly Sins, which once again distract Faustus from his doubts.

- In his study, Faustus tells Mephistopheles he will repent.
- The Good and Evil Angels offer encouragement and it appears Faustus can almost hear the words of the latter.
- Faustus accepts that he is damned and then asks Mephistopheles questions about the universe.
- When Mephistopheles refuses to answer about the creator of the world, Faustus wavers once again.
- The Good and Evil Angels reappear and Faustus cries out to Christ, at which point Lucifer and Beelzebub appear to intervene.
- Lucifer shows Faustus the Seven Deadly Sins.
- Faustus accepts another book and is pacified once more.

There is something childlike about Faustus's ability to be soothed by shows and books. For an intelligent academic, he is easily swayed by superficial matters. With the benefit of dramatic irony (the audience know he is doomed), viewers are more focused on the ways in which he is duped.

The Angels appear in the moments where Faustus is in doubt and, while they may be a personification of his uncertainty, in this scene it seems as if he can hear the Evil Angel. In **morality plays**, the Sins were often paraded before protagonists to prick their conscience. In this scene, they seem little more than an entertaining distraction rather than a wake-up call. Faustus doesn't realise that the Sins are part of a strategy of damning rather than saving him.

> **asides** lines delivered to the audience that cannot be heard by other characters
>
> **morality plays** medieval plays in which symbolic characters such as Virtue and Vice competed for the attention of the central character

Activity 6

Look closely at the detail of the scene and make notes on the following points:

- what makes Faustus change his mind about salvation in the line **'My heart's so hardened I cannot repent'**
- why Mephistopheles will not answer questions about Creation when he says **'I will not'**
- why Lucifer appears when he does
- why Lucifer might want Faustus to watch the show of the Seven Deadly Sins: **'… examine them of their several names and dispositions'**.

Act III Chorus

Wagner takes the role of the Chorus at the beginning of Act III. He fills in some details about Faustus's travels and looks forward to the next part of the story. The function here is to provide a bridge between the Faustus of the previous scenes, who in some ways is an observer of magic, and the character in Acts 4 and 5, who is a much more active performer of magical deeds.

- Wagner tells the audience that Faustus has ascended Mount Olympus from where he surveys the skies.
- We learn that after travelling the globe on a dragon-driven chariot, Faustus then travels to Rome.

This is usually the first scene performed after the interval in the theatre and it does signify a shift in the play. Part of this is to do with setting; the first two acts occur in smaller settings, often Faustus's study. Wagner's recount of Faustus's travels introduces a global element and prepares for scenes set in European courts.

Activity 7

Compare the tone of Wagner's words at the beginning of Act III with those in the Prologue. Which speech seems more moralistic and judgmental? Why do you think this is?

Act III Scene I

This scene takes place at the Pope's court in Rome and in performance lends itself to action and spectacle, with a disguise being worn, a trick being played and a succession of powerful characters thronging the stage.

- In fairly lengthy exchanges of dialogue, Faustus and Mephistopheles recount their journey through Europe.
- They have arrived in Rome on the day of Peter's feast and plan to disrupt the event.
- Mephistopheles places a robe on Faustus, making him invisible.
- A procession enters, including the Pope and the Cardinal of Lorraine. A banquet is brought in.
- Faustus plays a succession of tricks – whispering, stealing meat and wine, and hitting the Pope on the head.
- The Friars sing a dirge and Faustus and Mephistopheles beat them.

You might think that original audiences of the play would be horrified at Faustus's disregard for religious authority, but at this point in history England was essentially a Protestant country and the Pope, as leader of the Catholic Church, was viewed with disdain by many. Faustus's trick is usually endorsed by audiences, keeping them on his side even though he is clearly treading a very dangerous path.

As with most comedy, the scene works on the control of knowledge. The lack of awareness of the Cardinal and Friars, and then the Pope's inability to realise what is happening, creates much humour. The audience has the same knowledge as Faustus and Mephistopheles, so once again we are invited to side with them, laughing along with the pranks.

Activity 8

The relationship between Faustus and Mephistopheles seems closer in this scene, almost like a double act. How does Marlowe show this?

Act III Scene II

This is another comic scene, which parallels events in the Faustus storyline. The positioning of this scene seems odd in terms of the time sequence, as it seems to follow shortly after Act II Scene II, yet the appearance of Mephistopheles from Constantinople implies that the scene occurs much later, after the world trip has commenced.

- Robin and Rafe have stolen a silver goblet from the inn and are chased by the Vintner.
- Laughter ensues as the cup is swapped while the Vintner searches them.
- Mephistopheles enters to chastise Robin and Rafe, turning Robin into an ape and Rafe into a dog.

The humour is visual in nature, with the comic business of the swapping of the cup reliant upon the physical aspect of farce. Likewise, the transformation of Robin and Rafe is played for laughs. There is an echo of the previous scene here, playing on Faustus's misbehaviour at the banquet.

Activity 9

Look back over Act III. How do you respond to the following two views about it?

In Act III, Faustus is presented as a daring and sympathetic character.

Act III is more interesting to watch than it is to read.

Act IV Chorus

This brief speech provides information about the next phase of Faustus's travels. It also allows some convenient time in performance for scene changes.

- After his visit to the Pope, Faustus has returned home, where his friends have missed his presence.
- Faustus amazes his companions with tales of his feats and the Chorus then explains that Faustus is heading to the court of Emperor Charles V.

Act IV Scene I

The opening scene of this act is set at Emperor Charles's court in Germany and further confirms the trivial ways in which Faustus uses his powers. The tone of the play appears to shift away from seriousness and more towards farce, yet the seemingly superficial events hold some symbolic meanings too.

A further character is introduced in this scene – the Horse-courser, whose job as a trader of horses was often looked upon with disdain. In his deal with Faustus, he clearly thinks he has the upper hand.

- Charles and attendants enter. Charles asks Faustus to raise the spirits of Emperor Alexander and his paramour; their spirits enter.
- The Knight (who has been critical of Faustus) is given horns, which are subsequently removed.
- Faustus sells his horse to the Horse-courser for what seems a low price.
- Faustus warns the courser not to take the horse through water.
- Faustus briefly reflects on his position.
- Faustus sleeps and the courser re-enters – the horse has turned into a bottle (a bundle) of hay.
- Faustus remains asleep and the courser pulls off the Doctor's leg, which reappears after the courser exits.

The spectacular nature of the events here makes for great theatre, blending the pomp of the emperor's court with ghostly appearances of historical figures and the sexual joke about Benvolio wearing the cuckold's horns. For some readers, the act distracts from the tragic seriousness of Faustus's downfall.

Charles's fascination with the vision of Alexander offers an echo of Faustus's compulsive regard for magic. A further parallel is offered in the reference to Actaeon made by Faustus, a tale of a man so obsessed with an image – that of the goddess Diana – that he is torn apart. In both cases, the concept of a man being consumed by something that might destroy him has an obvious parallel to Faustus's obsession with necromancy.

The image on the title page of 'An Answer to the London Cuckold'

The cuckold's horns

A cuckold is a man whose wife has been unfaithful. The public humiliation of this is represented in the metaphorical wearing of cuckold's horns, a symbol that represents the supposedly lustful ram.

Activity 10

a) Read the panel on the cuckold's horns and then research the myth of Diana and Actaeon.

b) Look back to Act II Scene III and Act III Scene II, which both involve transformation and references to cuckoldry. Why might the play contain references to changing appearances, death and infidelity? How does this link to overall ideas in the play?

Act IV Scene II

This scene shows Faustus back among more privileged society, which presumably takes place at the Duke of Vanholt's court. More visual trickery occurs in this scene.

- The pregnant Duchess of Vanholt asks Faustus to produce some grapes.
- Faustus does so and receives an unspecified reward for his conjuring.

Views about Act IV

For some readers, Act IV is nothing more than a rapid, entertaining farce that distracts from the tragic trajectory found elsewhere in the play. However, it is possible to see a wider meaning in the events whereby some of the moral messages that emerge link to ideas about sin and Faustus's experience.

Here are some possible moral messages that emerge from Act IV:

- Human beings can be distracted by things that appear superficially attractive.
- Even powerful and intelligent people can be fooled.
- Humans make rash decisions that they live to regret.
- Powerful people enjoy exercising their authority.
- Public humiliation is worse than death.
- Pride comes before a fall.
- Humans should know their place and stay within their capabilities.

Activity 11

Take the seven statements above and identify where these moral messages are represented in the events of Act IV. You could use a table like this:

Scene(s)	Explanation of...	Shown by...
Act IV Scene I	Human beings can be distracted by things that appear superficially attractive.	Charles's amazement at the spirit of Alexander and his paramour

> ## Activity 12
>
> Look again at statements you considered in Activity 11. Which ones accurately describe Faustus's experiences?

Act V Scene I

The final act returns the audience to Faustus's study and moves into a more tragic mode as Faustus's end nears. There has clearly been a passing of time. The action concerns the final chance for Faustus to repent.

- Wagner explains that Faustus has made his will and is feasting.
- Scholars enter and Faustus conjures up the spirit of Helen of Greece (also called Helen of Troy).
- The Old Man enters, imploring Faustus to repent.
- Faustus prepares to kill himself but the Old Man persuades him not to.
- An angry Mephistopheles tells Faustus to re-swear allegiance to Lucifer and Faustus does so, once again with his own blood.
- Faustus instructs Mephistopheles to torture the Old Man.
- Helen's spirit returns and Faustus kisses her.

The entrance of the Old Man is crucial to this scene; not only is he an embodiment of the views of the Good Angel, but his presence changes the way we see Faustus. Quite who the Old Man is remains a mystery, yet he passionately implores Faustus to repent and, temporarily, it appears that the Doctor is on the brink of turning away from Lucifer. Faustus's rejection of the Old Man's advice seems a real error, but the cruelty of Faustus's request to harm him potentially destroys any sympathy the audience has for Faustus.

Helen is the final of the manifestations and, as with the images of Alexander and the Seven Deadly Sins, she reminds the audience of the distracting power of illusion. In her second appearance, Faustus is bewitched by her beauty, which belies the fact that she is associated with death and destruction. In kissing a spirit, Faustus damns himself.

> ### Key quotations
>
> **Ah, stay, good Faustus, stay thy desperate steps!**
> *(Old Man)*
>
> **Revolt, or I'll in piecemeal tear thy flesh.**
> *(Mephistopheles)*
>
> **Was this the face that launched a thousand ships**
> **And burnt the topless towers of Ilium?**
> *(Faustus)*

Activity 13

Research the various mythical references in Faustus's speech about Helen in Act V Scene I from **'Was this the face...'** to **'... thou shalt be my paramour'**. Note the links to war and destruction.

Act V Scene II

This scene shows the death of Faustus. As is common in tragedy, the protagonist is given a soliloquy to acknowledge his actions and express his despair.

- The Scholars implore Faustus to repent. He confesses his pact with Lucifer.

- The Scholars leave and Faustus reflects on his fate.

- Lucifer, Mephistopheles and the Devils enter. Faustus is taken away.

In some tragedies, when death comes it is a private experience. In this scene, the diabolical forces appear and one of the key debates in tragedy emerges: to what extent is the individual to blame for his own downfall?

Faustus's final soliloquy is one of absolute terror. The use of clocks and watches to remind both him and the audience of the inescapability of fate provides real drama as he scrabbles around for ways to escape his fate. His final offer of burning his books is futile, but may suggest an awareness that the pursuit of knowledge is at the root of his tragedy.

Helen of Troy (1898) by Evelyn de Morgan

Key quotations

Now hast thou but one bare hour to live *(Faustus)*

Ugly hell, gape not. Come not, Lucifer!
I'll burn my books. Ah, Mephistopheles! *(Faustus)*

Activity 14

Read the dialogue between Faustus and the Scholars. What is being suggested about blame here? Where do the sympathies of the Scholars lie? Find some quotations that show their attitudes towards Faustus's situation.

Activity 15

Explore Faustus's final soliloquy, taking careful note of his thought processes. List the ways he considers to try to avoid death.

Epilogue

The final scene of the Epilogue, like many tragedies, functions as a reflection on the death of the protagonist.

- The Chorus enters, urging the audience to learn from Faustus's errors.

You will notice how the words of the Chorus offer a moral to the audience and summarise Faustus's story.

> **Key quotation**
>
> **Cut is the branch that might have grown full straight** (Chorus)

Activity 16

How do you react to these views of the Chorus's words?

> The Chorus's words offer no sympathy for Faustus.

> The Chorus's words seem quite threatening towards the audience and end the play in a flat way.

> The Chorus's words accurately reflect the way that audiences see Faustus's story.

> The Chorus's description of Faustus's story is reductive and ignores his brilliance.

Tips for assessment

Knowing the text really well allows you the freedom to select the very best quotations and references to explain the point you are making. Students who are unsure of parts of the text often rely on the scenes they know best, even if they are not very relevant to the question. This means their answer will not be as good as it could be.

Structure

Exploring the structure of a text is different from focusing simply on the events of the play. When you explore the plot, you are considering the events that happen. When you think about structure, you are thinking about the order and manner in which those events are revealed to the audience.

Tragic structure

In **dramatic tragedy**, a key decision or error of judgment leads to further problems and usually death. *Doctor Faustus* is shaped by two key events: Faustus's pact with Lucifer and his final demise. But the play is much more than that. There are elements of the morality play, which you will explore in the Genre chapter. There are also scenes of farce. The play contains many symbolic figures, which gives it the feel of an **allegory**, and the settings range from the enclosed study of Faustus to various courts of Europe.

A key part of the sequence is the use of a Chorus, which initially provides the backstory of Faustus and his studies, but the dramatic focus of the play is on the Doctor's journey to death. The structure of drama usually moves through **complication** to **catastrophe** to **resolution**. In dramatic tragedy, there is often a restoration of order. The closing scene sometimes offers a sense of optimism that evilness is cut away and a more settled world can begin.

> **allegory** a story in which the characters have symbolic meaning
>
> **catastrophe** the climactic moment when disaster strikes
>
> **complication** an event that intensifies an existing conflict
>
> **dramatic tragedy** a play showing the suffering and demise of the protagonist
>
> **resolution** the part of a story where problems are resolved

Activity 17

Using the plot summaries in the first part of this chapter, identify:

- the initial problem(s) in the early scenes
- the types of conflicts experienced by each character
- where the complications occur and how they develop the problems
- the positioning of climactic moments
- which events bring about the resolution.

You could use a diagram such as a flow chart or spider diagram to help you map out the events and make links between them.

Activity 18

Look closely at the Epilogue. Is there any sense of optimism?

The balance between seriousness and farce

Some dramas contain story strands that may be termed 'plot' and 'subplot'. Although it's possible to see how serious events in *Doctor Faustus* are ironically paralleled by comic servant scenes, the links between the comic scenes aren't substantial enough to deem them a subplot. For instance, the theft of the Pope's dish is echoed by the theft of the Vintner's goblet, but most of the comic scenes are just that – a light-hearted, farcical antidote to the more serious moments.

Yet as you explore the balance between the serious and light-hearted elements, you should consider if it is possible to categorise the play into 'serious scenes' and 'comic scenes'. For instance, in the 2011 Shakespeare's Globe production, the moment in Act I Scene III where Faustus casts his first spell has some light comedy – the Doctor's initial attempt fails, despite a dramatic build-up, causing the audience to laugh at the anticlimax.

Activity 19

a) Look again at the events in each scene and note the parts that deal with serious ideas and those that are comic. You could use a table like this:

Act / Scene	Serious elements	Comic elements
I.1		

b) What is the balance between serious and comic moments in the play? Is it too simplistic to say that the Faustus scenes deal with serious matters and the other scenes are comic?

Time

The handling of time in the play is worth considering. The play offers a biographical journey over 24 years compressed into a two-hour play. As you will have noticed in the Prologue, the Chorus gives a rapid account of Faustus's upbringing and early career, and the initial phase of the play where the Doctor learns to conjure contains a few time shifts. One of the functions of the Chorus is to cover the passing of years with a summary. Matters such as Faustus's eight-day exploration on the back of a dragon are dealt with in a matter of lines.

The middle section of the play offers snapshots of Faustus's actions, but the most interesting use of time occurs in Act V Scene II, where Faustus's final soliloquy fits the course of an hour in the world of the play. It's here where the structural device of time feeds into a tragic theme of the play: Faustus's inevitable death is subject to time. Time is another wider force beyond his control.

Activity 20

Explore the passing of time in Act V Scene II, taking careful note of the points in the scene where time is signalled by clocks and watches.

Structural issues

The middle section of the play presents a problem for some members of the audience, especially Act IV, because it appears to take the drama away from the central story of Faustus's developing tragedy and the play is fleshed out with light-hearted scenes. Some critics have argued that by placing Faustus's decision to sell his soul near the beginning of the narrative, Marlowe leaves a large gap in the middle of the play. While the audience waits for his inevitable destruction, Marlowe fills the middle acts with farce and other matters that distract from the tragedy. However, the middle sequence of the play is essential as it reveals just how limited and superficial Faustus's actions become. His showy antics are part of the tragedy – a doomed man distracting himself with fripperies.

Activity 21

How do you react to these two views of the play's structure?

> The play is a dazzlingly brilliant amalgam of genres, times and places. Part of the entertainment comes from the variety the play provides.

> The play is structurally loose – it is more a collection of dramatic scenes than a coherent story.

Writing about structure

Exploring the larger structural features of a story, such as where and how the action starts, how the resolution of the play is brought about and, crucially, when the characters – and audience – discover key information will help you to see the ways in which Marlowe has shaped the narrative. The ability to analyse the structural features of a text will give your answers much more depth and quality.

Studying the context of a piece of literature can mean thinking about the surrounding beliefs and cultural ideas that existed at the time of production, i.e. when the work was written. You should also consider how your own personal contexts in the world you live in affect how you might read and interpret a play. When deciding on how you view *Doctor Faustus,* the contexts of reception (the point where you personally 'receive' or experience the play) can be as revealing as historical context.

Some modern approaches to literature avoid trying to second-guess 'what the author meant' and prefer to consider how the reader interprets the text. Whether it is ever possible to work out 'what Marlowe intended' by writing the play is doubtful, but it is certainly possible to say how *you* interpret it as a 21st-century reader. Find out how the course you are studying regards context: are you required to

Christopher Marlowe (1564–93)

apply historical contexts to the play, or are cultural and literary contexts preferred? Use the following material to help shape your thoughts about the various contextual backdrops against which you can judge the play.

Marlowe's beliefs

You need to be careful when using biographical information about writers, because it can sometimes detract from close analysis of the text. Giving details about a writer's life is only useful if it sheds light on the literature you are studying. You should also be aware that while the concerns of authors and playwrights obviously inform their subject matter not everything a writer presents is an embodiment of their firmly held beliefs. For instance, many accounts of Marlowe's life present him as an atheist and yet you might read *Doctor Faustus* as being a play that urges people to follow the teachings of the Bible or risk damnation.

Used wisely, Marlowe's beliefs and life may help shed some light on the meanings of the play. Although he died before he was 30, Marlowe's life and plays attracted controversy. Reputedly a spy who lost his life in a tavern brawl, Marlowe was accused of heresy, supposedly saying that religion's purpose was 'to keep men in awe.

The English Faust Book

Today, literary works are expected to be original. In Marlowe's time, writers usually adapted existing stories. The story Marlowe uses as his source was first published in England in 1592 as *The English Faust Book*, yet it originated in Germany in 1587. It is based on a historical figure who supposedly made a pact with the devil. Many of the scenes from the play are found in *The English Faust Book* and it is tempting to imagine how a story about rejecting God may have struck a chord with the supposedly heretical Marlowe.

Activity 1

Read through the digitised pages of *The English Faust Book* on the British Library website. Look particularly at the contents page to see the links between the original text and the events in Marlowe's play.

Activity 2

Read the following extract from *The English Faust Book*. It is an account of the scene where the Old Man speaks to Faustus. Read it alongside Act V Scene I. What are the similarities and differences between this version and Marlowe's dramatisation of the scene? Start by considering the content of the Old Man's speech and the manner in which he addresses Faustus in Act V Scene I.

He invited Doctor *Faustus* to supper into his house, unto the which he agreed and having ended their banquet, the old man began with these words: 'My loving friend and neighbour Doctor *Faustus*, I have to desire of you a friendly and Christian request, beseeching you that you will vouchsafe not to be angry with me, but friendly resolve me in my doubt, and take my poor inviting in good part.' To whom Doctor Faustus answered: 'My loving neighbour, I pray you say your mind.'

Then began the old Patron to say: 'My good neighbour, you know in the beginning how that you have defied God and all the host of heaven and given your soul to the Devil, wherewith you have incurred God's high displeasure, and are become from a Christian fare worse than a heathen person: oh consider what you have done, it is not only the pleasure of the body, but the safety of the soul that you must have respect unto: of which if you be careless, then are you cast away, and shall remain in the anger of almighty God.

(P. F. Gent, *The Historie of the Damnable Life and Deserved Death of Doctor John Faustus*, 1592)

Religious context

It is difficult to understand *Doctor Faustus* fully without some awareness of Christian beliefs and Bible stories. The material in the following sections gives an overview of religious contexts for reading the play, which you may choose to research further. However, make sure that you don't lose sight of the play at the expense of religious context: the following contextual ideas are all things that arise from the play. In the end, your prime text is the play itself, so make sure this is central to your studies. Use the following details about religion to illuminate your understanding.

Tips for assessment

When writing in the exam, don't be tempted to recount large chunks of context you may have researched, however interesting they may be. Brief references to historical or religious context should be linked directly to the text and should be made to help explain or explore Marlowe's dramatic choices.

Belief systems

Religious beliefs and systems at the time Marlowe was writing weren't settled affairs, so don't assume that all original audience members thought and felt about religion in the same way.

During the 16th century, Western Christianity underwent a schism, in which prominent men such as Martin Luther and John Calvin broke away from the Catholic Church, which was led by the Pope. During this Protestant Reformation, and around 70 years before the play was performed, England was declared a Protestant country. This made the English monarch the figurehead of the Protestant Church of England, but even so, many people remained Catholic and Catholic beliefs were still widespread.

These competing versions of Christianity are echoed in the play and, while there are some anti-Catholic scenes (the mockery of the Pope, for instance), debates around predestination and free will were still active. Some people thought that God had set out (predestined) a pattern for every human life, crucially determining from the outset whether a person is destined to be 'saved' (i.e. will enter heaven upon their death) or not; others believed that human beings have free will, the ability to decide their own path in life (rather than it being determined by God).

Catholic religious beliefs and practices

Many beliefs and practices of the Catholic Church were embedded in the 16th-century world. Here are some of them:

- A person's sins and good deeds were counted up at the end of their life by a heavenly force.

- The difference between evil and good acts would inform how long the person spent in purgatory, a place where sins were purged (got rid of by physical torment).

- Almost everyone went through purgatory, but the time spent could be reduced by saying prayers for your own (and other people's) soul. God would accept those who repented.

- Humans had free will – some control over the pattern of their life and their path through life.

Calvinist religious beliefs and practices

By the end of the 16th century in England, the beliefs of John Calvin were the dominating version of Protestantism in England. Here are some of them:

- Life was predestined: God decided at the beginning of the world how many people would enter heaven and how many would be sent to hell.

- Humans didn't know whether they were destined for heaven or hell – only God did.

- A person's depth of faith was perhaps a good measure of where they were heading in the afterlife.

Activity 3

Read the information panels about Catholic and Calvinist beliefs carefully. Does *Doctor Faustus* present a world in which free will is championed or do the actions in the play imply that life is predestined? As a starting point, consider the following excerpts from the play:

- **The reward of sin is death.** (*Faustus, Act I Scene I*)

- **Faustus, repent yet, God will pity thee.** (*Good Angel, Act II Scene III*)

- **I see an angel hovers o'er thy head,**
  And with a vial full of precious grace
  Offers to pour the same into thy soul. (*Old Man, Act V Scene I*)

- **Let Faustus live in hell a thousand years,**
  A hundred thousand, and at last be saved. (*Faustus, Act V Scene II*)

The Great Chain of Being

Today, many cultures believe that humans should be able to progress and develop to be the best they can be. For others, traces of a class or caste system persist, which means that people think that their position in society is fixed.

Belief in a strict social order was common in Elizabethan England. The Great Chain of Being was a way of classifying all the things purported to exist. This meant a taxonomy (the practice and science of classification) stretching from God at the top right down to liquids and metals. Of all the things on Earth, man was highest and above man were the angels and then God. Although it was recognised that man had the ability to think and feel, religious teachings advocated than man should use these abilities to learn about God rather than to demystify the universe.

The Great Chain of Being was hierarchical and implied that the world was fixed and that any attempt to rise above one's position was effectively a slight against God. Faustus's desires are quite clearly in opposition to such beliefs and would have been deemed a threat to the order and stability of life, and by extension, the will of God. The roots of these beliefs are found in the Bible (also referred to as scripture), most notably the story of Adam.

Adam and pride

The story of Adam's temptation in the Bible has obvious echoes with Faustus's ambition. You will notice that the Chorus appears to remind the audience to know their place, rather than practising **'more than heavenly power permits'** (Chorus, Epilogue). In some readings of the play, the Epilogue reinforces Christian teachings and echoes the moral of the Garden of Eden story, which implies that humans should not aspire to the role of God.

The closing lines of the play offer an interpretation that instructs the audience to **'Regard his hellish fall'** (Chorus, Epilogue) – in other words, take notice of Faustus's fate and learn **'only to wonder'** (Chorus, Epilogue) at those things that tempt us, rather than act upon our desires. It draws attention to the corrupted nature of the protagonist: he is **'Cut'** and **'burnèd'** (Chorus, Epilogue). The idea of humans knowing their limits is a recurring one in Western literature, with the assumption that the power of God as envisaged by scripture outweighed the desires of man.

Activity 4

Read the account of Adam and The Fall opposite.

a) What parallels do you see in Faustus's story?

b) Consider how both stories present obedience, power, temptation and punishment.

Adam and The Fall

In Genesis, the first book of the Bible, the story of Adam's temptation explores how man disobeys God, with dire consequences. Having been gifted a paradise to dwell in – the Garden of Eden – God instructs Adam and Eve not to eat from the Tree of Knowledge of Good and Evil. Eve is tempted by a serpent to eat an apple from the tree. She then tempts Adam, who also succumbs. An angry God casts Adam and Eve out of the Garden of Eden.

This event is known as The Fall – the lapse in judgement that means, from that point on, humanity is said to live in a postlapsarian state (the state of lost innocence), one in which we are all sinners. The image of the prelapsarian paradise (a metaphorical paradise of a state of innocence) is common to many pastoral narratives and embodies the time of innocence often symbolised in the image of the Garden of Eden – an unspoilt time before man's original sin.

Adam and Eve (1526) by Lucas Cranach

Adam's sin in this story is one of pride – the excessive self-belief that makes people assume that their knowledge and skills are more assured than anyone else's. In the story of Adam, God's superior knowledge and guidance is ignored. Adam's story is also echoed in the story of Lucifer's rebellion in heaven, as referred to in the play by Mephistopheles. Pride is usually regarded as the root of all sins.

Doctor Faustus and your own beliefs

If you accept that meanings of texts change over time because societies and their social and cultural beliefs change, then you will see how your own 21st-century religious belief, or lack of belief, informs how you judge the play. Some readers will approach *Doctor Faustus* from a secular point of view not connected with religious or spiritual matters, assuming that Lucifer and God don't exist, and therefore they will view the play as one that explores how an ambitious academic is caught up in old belief systems. If you follow a religion that advocates that accepting God's authority is essential, then you might well see Faustus as a man who deserves censure.

Activity 5

Explore how your own beliefs affect your responses to the play. Which, if any, of these statements do you agree with?

> The play shows how selfish and conceited man is. Just like Adam and countless others after him, Faustus assumes that he is allowed to attain knowledge he has no right to. The play serves as a reminder that there is a cosmic order in the world and that humans need to remember their place in the grand scheme of things

> *Doctor Faustus* shows the suffocating qualities of religion that seek to constrain natural curiosity. The rules of religion run counter to human interest, so the play shows how the repressive nature of beliefs lead to disaster: it's not man that is the problem – it's the arbitrary nature of religion and the way in which the Church uses stories to control people.

> The text offers an interesting insight into the clash between various types of belief. In the play, there are elements of both Catholic and Calvinist beliefs, as well as belief in the power of the individual and the power of evil.

The Renaissance and the individual

From around 1350, a major growth in cultural and academic matters flourished in Europe for a period of 250 years. It was later termed the Renaissance ('rebirth') and marked a change in the way humans saw their place in the world. Scholarship was prized and the intellectual life of Europe benefited from developments in a range of areas, such as astronomy, physics, art and literature. The centrality of the individual was also endorsed by events during this period. It was a time of self-discovery and the desire to learn more about all facets of existence.

Challenges to scientific beliefs were proposed by figures such as Galileo and Copernicus. Painting techniques developed and artists attempted to capture more realistic depictions of their subjects. Developments in navigation meant that travel became easier and so, in many ways, the Renaissance was the age of discovery. The rest of the world came closer to home through the efforts of humans, most notably those individuals such as Francis Drake who circumnavigated the globe during the middle of the 16th century.

Rather than simply following the beliefs of the medieval Church without critical evaluation, the Renaissance celebrated the ability of man to engage with complex concepts and ideas from Roman and Greek cultures, which often led to a questioning of accepted thought. The development of the printing press in the middle of the 15th century, coupled with the translation of the Bible into common English (rather than Latin), meant people could access scripture for themselves.

Activity 6

Read the dialogue between Faustus and Mephistopheles at the start of Act II Scene III.

a) How does Mephistopheles explain the nature of the world? Does it fit with your current understanding of the way the world is organised?

b) Why might Mephistopheles refuse to answer Faustus's question about the creation of the world?

Renaissance man and the over-reacher

The concept of the 'Renaissance man' persists today as the embodiment of the person who has a range of interests and strengths – a polymath who sees the acquisition of knowledge from lots of disciplines as an indication of human achievement. In the 16th century, Nicolaus Copernicus was best known in the field of astronomy but he was also a doctor and lawyer. The poet John Donne was also an MP, Royal Chaplain and Dean of St Paul's Cathedral.

The elevation of the individual and the ability of humans to excel is one that is familiar to many 21st-century readers too, yet with it comes caution. It is a short step between unswerving self-belief and the arrogance that can lead to disaster. The fatal flaw of **hubris** features in many stories across the ages and is echoed in the story of Icarus mentioned earlier.

The literary concept of the overreacher – the character who reaches beyond their limits – can be applied to Faustus. As you will see in the next chapter, tragic stories very often deal with protagonists whose failure to acknowledge boundaries results in death. Shakespeare's Macbeth is a character whose ambition leads him to commit regicide and Shelley's Dr Frankenstein steals body parts from the dead in order to create life. These are narratives that advise the reader to stay within accepted limits of human conduct.

You will notice how many of the concepts in this chapter intertwine: the overreacher is a version of Adam, the character who disobeyed the rules laid down for him. But you will also see how the values of scripture and the values of the Renaissance sit uneasily alongside each other at times. On one hand, religious teachings suggest that man needs to accept God's law, whereas the flowering of individual thought in the Renaissance appears to endorse the strides of humanity to push boundaries further than ever.

hubris excessive pride, which leads characters to ignore warnings and presume that they know best

Activity 7

Look again at the Prologue and take note of the way the Chorus presents Faustus's story as a clash between individual self-belief and the heavens.

a) Which phrases express this clash?

b) Does the Chorus favour Faustus or the heavens? Explain why you think this.

Magic

To most modern readers, magic is associated with illusion and stagecraft. A true belief in magic is unusual in the 21st century and seen in opposition to science and also religion. However, in Marlowe's time, the distinction was less clear cut. The work of John Dee, a good example of a Renaissance man, sought to harness the power of nature and supernatural knowledge to purify the lives of humans; a symbolic attempt to return them to a prelapsarian state.

Men such as Dee and Cornelius Agrippa (who wrote *De Occulta Philosophia* in 1531) saw 'white magic' as complementary to Christian belief. 'Black magic' was associated with superstition rather than science and Satan rather than Christ. The magic that Faustus practises invokes the devil and sits at odds with Dee's version, in spite of the fact that many commentators see John Dee as part of Marlowe's inspiration for Faustus.

Dr John Dee: scientist and magician

John Dee (1527–1609) may well have been the inspiration for the character of Doctor Faustus. As the owner of one of the largest libraries in Britain, his reputation as a bibliophile preceded him and contributed to the infamy he experienced in his own lifetime.

Dee was not only a well-known astronomer across Europe, he was also a mathematician, spy and necromancer. He was viewed as a **magus** figure and brilliant scholar. He provided scientific advice and information to Queen Elizabeth I and also had deeply spiritual qualities.

His desire for knowledge knew few bounds. Much like other ambitious, intelligent men, he desired to know more about the world, even if would lead to danger.

A portrait of Dr John Dee

magus a magician or sorcerer

Activity 8

Read the information about John Dee opposite. What links can you find between John Dee's life and works and those of Faustus? You could use a table like the one below to record the links.

John Dee	Doctor Faustus
Has mastered a range of skills such as astronomy, maths, etc.	Is also a polymath – appears to have mastered law, divinity, etc.

Activity 9

Bearing in mind the contextual information in this chapter, how do you regard the meanings of the play? Which, if any, of the following statements describing the play seem closest to your understanding of *Doctor Faustus*?

- A play criticising religion
- A play criticising excessive human desire
- A play celebrating human ambition
- A play exploring the clash of belief systems

Writing about context

Be careful not to deal with context in a generalised way. Although it's possible to talk about the general beliefs held by Elizabethans, avoid making sweeping statements that assume that all Elizabethans accepted the social structure of the day, for example. As a comparison, you might think about all of the people you know and consider whether their views can be lumped together as 'what 21st-century people think' or whether people have a variety of viewpoints regardless of the times in which they live.

It's always best to couch any points you make about context in tentative terms and let the contextual material arise naturally from the play, rather than 'force' contexts on the play. Simply expressing some facts about contexts of production will not add much to your writing. Any writing about context should be linked to the events of the play, as shown in this section of the book. Using these methods in your own writing will help you to handle context effectively.

Genre

One very important context against which *Doctor Faustus* can be read is that of literary genre. Genre refers to the text type or category a piece of writing can be placed in. By putting a label on a text, readers begin to interpret them – they come to expect certain events and actions to occur. One way to view *Doctor Faustus* is as a morality play. Another way is to categorise the play as tragedy.

Morality plays

Morality plays were popular from around 1400 but from 1580 they fell out of popularity. As the name implies, they were dramas that explored aspects of human conduct and, in essence, aimed to guide audiences to follow a moral path. The action itself wasn't simply a pious sermon; the drama often contained lewd behaviour and vulgarity, and a range of entertaining scenes.

The moral messages of these plays reinforced Christian teachings and explored the human condition, rather than attempting to develop complex characters as later dramatists did. Central characters were a representation of humanity, as seen in the **eponymous** character in *Everyman*, who stood as a recognisable character embodying the common traits and attitudes of ordinary people.

Other characters in morality plays tended to be abstract personifications. For instance, in *The Castle of Perseverance*, figures such as The World, The Devil and The Seven Deadly Sins appear. The storylines of morality plays often involve the central character being tempted by characters such as Vice, but the ending of these plays showed the character turning to God and salvation.

> **eponymous** referring to a character whose name is also the title of the text

Activity 1

Read the plot summary of *Everyman* opposite. What temptations and challenges does the central character face? Can you see any parallels with *Doctor Faustus*?

Faustus is confronted by Lucifer

Everyman

Summoned by Death to go with him to meet God, Everyman asks for an extra day. Death says that's not possible, so Everyman seeks someone to travel with him. Initially, he finds Fellowship but is soon abandoned by him. His family abandon him too, as does Goods. He finds Accompaniment but, in the end, only Good Deeds remain, which suggests that it is only our good deeds that are of any worth in the face of death. An Angel receives Everyman and Good Deeds into heaven, and the play closes with a wise Doctor who explains to the audience that only man's good deeds will count. He also says that if man confesses his sins and evil deeds, God will save him.

Woodcut from the title page of *Everyman*

Conventions of the morality play

Genres have loose conventions or elements that are used or adapted by writers. In general, morality plays have the following features:

- The protagonist is a representation of an 'ordinary' person – someone with whom the audience can identify.
- The protagonist has many positive qualities but lacks fulfilment.
- A character(s) offers temptation and the protagonist gives in.
- The cast list contains a blend of realistic characters and abstract personifications.
- Good and evil forces are in a contest for control of the central character during the course of the plot.
- The storyline involves a journey, which can be a metaphor for the journey of life.
- There are scenes of evil behaviour and general riotousness, often for the purposes of comedy.
- The protagonist is regularly reminded of the need for restraint and godliness.
- The wisdom of a mentor figure is heeded.
- In the end, the protagonist returns to God and is saved.

Activity 2

a) Using the ten-point list on page 35, explore how far *Doctor Faustus* adheres to morality play conventions. Identify where in the play these elements occur. You could use a table like this:

Morality play	How *Doctor Faustus* follows or does not follow the convention
1	Faustus is 'base of stock' so represents everyday people; he is also a gifted academic so unlike most of the audience. People can relate to his frustration in a general sense, but his ambitions are unlike those of ordinary backgrounds.

b) Based on your findings, how far is the term 'morality play' an apt description of *Doctor Faustus*? In your opinion, which are the most significant changes Marlowe makes to the morality genre?

Doctor Faustus as tragedy

The term 'tragedy' is commonly used to describe sad events that occur in everyday life. However, in literature, tragedy is a stylised representation of suffering with a set of recognisable conventions. Tragedy dramatises how the actions of characters and fate bring about disastrous outcomes, usually death.

The first tragedies were written by Greek dramatists such as Euripides and featured the collapse of societies and great people. Shakespeare took some of the conventions of these dramas but also developed them, producing tragic plays such as *King Lear* and *Hamlet*. Both of these texts explore how important people make errors of judgement, or how they are conspired against, and subsequently contribute to their own demise.

In spite of its sombre subject matter, dramatic tragedy brings pleasure to the audience, as well as provoking pity. In watching the succession of dire events, pleasure is derived from the way in which the play unfolds and in the artistic quality of the language. Strong emotions are aroused, and it is possible that viewers receive an education of some sort – they are given the opportunity to reflect upon the more difficult aspects of human existence.

Actors perform on a giant clock face at the Staatsoper Unter den Linden theatre, Berlin, in the 2006 opera *Faustus, The Last Night*, based on Marlowe's play

Activity 3

Research the literary history of tragedy. Read summaries of early tragedies by playwrights such as Sophocles and later dramatists such as Ibsen and Miller.

a) What links do you find between the plots of early tragedy and the events of *Doctor Faustus*?

b) What are the significant differences between the status of the characters in Marlowe's play and those in more modern tragedies?

The conventions of tragedy

Although there are many different types of tragedy and the genre varies over time, there is a loose set of conventions that comprise literary tragedy. These can include the following:

- a plot that features a central protagonist who appears to have a weakness or flaw that drives their actions
- a protagonist who, either through their own actions or that of fate, suffers and loses status
- a sense of inevitability about the protagonist's downfall
- a villain or external force that threatens the protagonist
- a protagonist who does things that may be viewed as wrong, yet retains sympathy from the audience
- episodes of violence, disorder and suffering
- the death of the protagonist as a way to solve problems set up in the play
- a sense that order is restored at the very end of the play.

Activity 4

Using the eight-point list above, explore how far *Doctor Faustus* adheres to these conventions. Identify where in the play these tragic elements occur. You could use a table like this:

Tragic element	How *Doctor Faustus* follows or does not follow the convention
I	The Doctor's weaknesses: his desire to learn about things that will damn him follows tragic convention.

Order and disorder

The structure of most tragedies shows a movement from order to disorder, with a form of order being restored by the end of the play. The early scenes of a play are usually concerned with revealing the sense of unity or outward success. Sometimes this is done through a court scene, where the regal characters' actions suggest stability and a productive community. In some tragedies, a pleasant domestic scene or some sort of victory is often used to signify order.

In the early phase of a tragedy, an event occurs (or a character enters) that brings disorder. This might be in the shape of a dilemma or information that emerges. It may also be something that is internal to the protagonist, which changes the direction of the play. The momentum of the remainder of the play is focused on the gradual unravelling of the situation to a point where order of some sort is re-established. This might be the death of the protagonist, which rids society of its ills, or the emergence of a new political order.

Activity 5

Explore the shape of the play's storyline in terms of order and disorder.

a) Is it possible to say that a sense of an ordered world is present in Act I Scene I?

b) Which events or persons bring disorder into the world of the text?

c) The death of Faustus is part of the restoration of order, but is there anything at the end of the play that suggests a more stable time is coming?

Aristotle, tragedy and *Doctor Faustus*

Aristotle (see the panel opposite) suggested that tragic protagonists have greatness, which marks them out as special in status or in significance. Faustus's position as a highly regarded academic gives him status, and the manner in which he conducts himself in Act I Scene I and most of Acts III and IV suggests that he is widely revered. In order for tragedy to arouse feelings of pity, horror and pleasure in the audience, tragic protagonists must have qualities that the audience can relate to. When the scope of the protagonist's suffering is greater than their error, pity results.

Aristotle applied specific terms to the pattern of protagonist's experiences. He suggested that tragic characters possess a pronounced self-belief, which makes them carry on with their actions in spite of warnings. This sort of pride he termed hubris. He called the protagonist's errors of judgement, or the specific action which leads to the downfall, **hamartia**. The moment when the protagonist becomes aware of the magnitude of their error is known as **anagnorisis**.

The term **peripeteia** describes the moment of catastrophe – the point when the downfall occurs. The audience's emotional response to the events, the shedding of the feelings of pity and terror that build up during the play, is given the term **catharsis**.

> **anagnorisis** a moment of recognition where the protagonist realises the significance of their mistake
>
> **catharsis** the emotional release felt by the audience, a sense of cleansing
>
> **hamartia** a mistake made by the protagonist, which leads to their downfall
>
> **peripeteia** a catastrophe undergone by the protagonist; a reversal of fortune

Activity 6

Is it possible to apply the terms 'hubris', 'hamartia', 'anagnorisis' and 'peripeteia' to the events of *Doctor Faustus*? Identify the points in the story where these moments seem applicable.

Aristotle

Aristotle (384–322 BCE), a Greek philosopher, scientist and thinker, offered an outline of tragedy in his text *Poetics*. He based his views on the play *Oedipus Rex* by Sophocles. The conventions he identified are regarded as significant and, to an extent, seem to have influenced Renaissance dramatists. Aristotle describes tragedy as a representation of a serious, complete action that has magnitude (significance and consequence) and arouses pity and fear in the audience, leading to the catharsis of these emotions.

Statue of Aristotle

Faustus as a tragic hero

Tragic heroes or protagonists are often represented as outsiders. They regularly find themselves pitted against the values of the world they are part of. There is frequently something admirable in their refusal to simply accept the way things are. Tragic heroes usually have a sense of self-worth bordering on arrogance. They are often flawed individuals, beset by recognisable human qualities such as ambition or jealousy.

Activity 7

Read the following descriptions of tragic heroes. Which of these accurately describe Faustus?

Tragic protagonists:

- have strongly independent qualities. They handle the problems they're faced with on their own and don't appear to trust the judgements of others. They seem unwilling to compromise

- come to realise that their efforts or beliefs will result in their death. They suffer during most of the play and reluctantly see that their way of life or their choices were wrong. In spite of this, they proceed with a sense of noble futility

- are destroyed by their own mistakes or some flaw in their character. They are also victims of tragic villains, or fate, or both

- provoke negative responses in the audience. Their actions cause revulsion and their arrogance can be an unattractive quality

- provoke positive responses in the audience. Their self-belief and grandeur can be heroic, their philosophical manner attractive and the scale of their suffering a cause for sympathy.

The tragic death

Death in tragic plays usually brings closure – the hero's demise brings about an end to suffering. Dramatic tragedy reveals how errors of judgement lead to isolation, suffering and death, but the death isn't always seen as deserved: usually, it provokes pity and there is often a communal lament for the fallen hero. As in some films, death scenes can be drawn out and accompanied by a soliloquy in which protagonists offer their thoughts on their own tragedy. The language is often elevated and stylised. Although the manner of death may be gory, the language has a philosophical beauty that continues to reaffirm the heroes' intellectual and emotional qualities, in spite of their crimes.

In Faustus's final speech, he knows his death is imminent. In tragedy, protagonists realise their fate is inescapable. One of the wider significances of the genre is that life is random and humans are at the mercy of fate or the cruelty of others. You might explore how this is reflected in the soliloquy in Act V Scene II.

The tragic experience of Faustus provokes a range of responses from different audiences. Tragedies, according to Aristotle, have profound effects on viewers. Aristotle's term 'catharsis' to describe an audience's reaction at the end of a tragedy is derived from medicine and means 'purgation' and, by extension, the emotional release felt by the audience.

Activity 8

What, if any, emotional reaction do you have to events at the end of the play? Consider these possible responses as a starting point:

> We feel sorrow for Faustus's death but see the justice of it. The audience learns the lessons of his actions. The main feeling is one of uplift.

> The overriding emotion is one of sympathy. Faustus's experiences challenge us emotionally and provoke us to extend our human sympathies. We are better human beings for having witnessed these horrible events.

> Watching tragedy evokes a sense that life is futile: *Doctor Faustus* shows the random, cruel nature of life, and the dominant feeling is that life is meaningless.

Activity 9

Is Faustus's death mourned at the end of the play? Is there any acknowledgement that his passing is a cause for sorrow? Explain your ideas.

Richard Burton as Faustus in the 1967 film adaptation

Doctor Faustus: morality play or tragedy?

As this chapter implies, there is some dispute over how best to classify the play. Some readers would define it as a tragedy that uses aspects of the morality play as a starting point to explore the concerns of Renaissance man. Whether you need to decide firmly how you classify the play is debatable – it is probably enough to know that, like most plays, it can comfortably be seen against several genres, and that is one of its interesting aspects.

Activity 10

Read the critical view of the play's generic aspects by Andrew Duxfield below and answer the following questions.

a) Why does Duxfield think our judgement on Faustus himself informs whether we see the play as a tragedy or morality play?

b) What does Faustus's 'Promethean aspiration' refer to?

c) Explain whether you think the ambiguity of genre is a good thing or not.

What we have, it seems, is a play that, to a large degree, can be shown to satisfy the generic criteria of both the Morality and the Tragedy forms. It is often the interpretation of Faustus's character that leads to a preference for one form or another; it is disapproval of Faustus's 'base physical desires' that leads some critics to interpret him as an example in the Morality tradition, and admiration of his 'Promethean aspiration' that leads others to interpret him as an entirely tragic figure. Marlowe seems to have actively encouraged this ambiguity by constructing *Faustus* in such a way that it can be argued as belonging to either of two different genres which each promote diametrically opposing views on its protagonist.

(A. Duxfield, '"Resolve me of all ambiguities": *Doctor Faustus* and the Failure to Unify', *Early Modern Literary Studies* Special Issue 16 (October, 2007)

Prometheus

In Greek mythology, Prometheus is a Titan (an early god). He is viewed as a sort of trickster who steals fire from Mount Olympus to give to mankind. For this, Zeus punishes him by chaining him to a rock where an eagle pecks away at his liver for eternity.

Ancient Greek painting of Zeus punishing Prometheus

Writing about genre

Relating the play to its genre will help you to get away from simply writing about the events of the play or the actions of the characters. Dealing with *Doctor Faustus* in terms of wider literary contexts will help you to bring a sharper focus to the points you make.

It is important to remember that writers don't write to a formula. Although you may be able to see the skeleton of genre in *Doctor Faustus*, when writing about the play as a tragedy avoid the temptation to simply spot tragic or morality play elements: try to get beyond the features and see what meanings emerge.

Placing the play against the backdrops of the morality play and tragedy will illuminate your analysis of how Marlowe uses, and plays with, the conventions of these genres. Be alert to how he challenges your expectations and plays with convention.

Characterisation and Roles

Some older critical approaches treat characters as if they are real people and explore the beliefs and psychology of characters as if they have a choice in what they do and say. While any study of characters needs to start from what is done and said by the characters on stage, it is essential to explore them as *constructs*. The playwright – in this case Marlowe – decides everything in terms of what appears on the page. Writing about characters is insightful when it looks at *how* characters are constructed, rather than just describing their actions.

There is a difference in writing about characters and writing about *characterisation*. The latter looks at the choices made by the dramatist and thinks more widely about the character in relation to character type, role and function in the text.

Tips for assessment

Stepping back and thinking about the choices made by the playwright is comparable to watching a film and thinking less about the things the characters do on-screen and more about what the director, scriptwriter, make-up artist, etc., decide to show. Drama is, of course, a special kind of text where different productions of plays can lend a different slant to character. Make sure you balance what is on the page with how it might translate on stage.

Main characters

Doctor Faustus

The play, like many tragedies, is centred on an eponymous protagonist, so it's likely that your response to Doctor John Faustus is linked to how you interpret the text as a whole. You will have noticed that we hear about Faustus before he enters the stage via the words of the Chorus in the Prologue, and his positive and negative qualities are outlined. The gist of the Prologue suggests we have a character whose success has gone to his head **'swoll'n with cunning of a self-conceit'** *(Chorus, Prologue)*.

In terms of Faustus's early life, Marlowe chooses to reveal his humble origins from **'parents base of stock'** *(Chorus, Prologue)* and his spectacular rise in the university world. In Act V Scene II, Faustus explains that he was in Wittenberg for 30 years and, given the 24 years of his life that the play spans, the implication is that he is in his twenties at the beginning of the play. The recognisable **archetype** of the bright young man who refuses to be bound by convention emerges. Before we encounter him, Faustus is established as an intelligent, ambitious and rebellious character.

> **archetype** a model of a character type

Activity 1

Reread the Prologue and make a list of the characteristics of Faustus introduced by the Chorus. Link these to specific quotations. You could use a table like the one below:

Faustus's qualities	Quotation
He contributed to the world of academia.	**The fruitful plot of scholarism graced** *(Chorus, Prologue).*

One of the key things you will need to explore is whether Faustus is a character who deserves your sympathy or whether you view him simply as the arrogant overreacher that the Chorus suggests. It is probable that your view will alter several times during the play, but you may feel that there exists a subtle tension between the view the Chorus offers and the character as he appears through his own words and actions.

The opening soliloquy in Act I Scene I suggests a man who seeks power. Marlowe shows us a man who has achieved fame from his ability to cure whole cities, but this isn't enough. He wants control of the Earth and what lies above it, seeking treasures and delights from all corners of the Earth. In essence, he is curious and exhibits the very traits that Adam gave in to. Yet, at the same time, he captures the spirit of the Renaissance man in his desire for further knowledge and achievement. He seeks to know the secrets of the universe, wishing that spirits will **'Resolve me of all ambiguities'** *(Act I Scene I).*

Jude Law as Faustus in the Young Vic production, 2002

Soliloquy invites the audience into the confidence of the protagonist so there is a tendency to assume that everything Faustus says in solo speech might be taken at face value. The Chorus has alerted us to the Doctor's shortcomings, however, so a close reading of Faustus's logic in Act I Scene I is needed because, in spite of claiming to have attained **'logic's chiefest end'** *(Faustus, Act I Scene I)*, some of his decision-making seems rash to say the least. Even before his fatal decision to enter into the pact, he reveals some flawed thinking based on the Scriptures.

Activity 2

In Act I Scene I, Faustus pronounces judgement on a line from Jerome's Bible, ironically claiming to **'view it well'**. The original phrase from the Bible is: 'the wages of sin is death, but the gift of God is eternal life' *(Romans 6: 23)*. How does the original compare to Faustus's rendering of it? What is being implied about the accuracy of Faustus's logic?

Activity 3

Look closely at Act I Scene I from **'How am I glutted...'** to '**... blest with your sage conference!'** In these lines Faustus expresses the things he wishes spirits to fetch. Which of these desires are personal and which are more universal in nature? How far is it fair to say that Faustus is self-seeking?

One of the motifs of the play is Faustus's wavering. His enthusiasm for necromancy is tempered by moments of doubt, which are in part expressed through the appearance of the Good and Evil Angels, but also through his own dialogue. Yet in each case, he allows himself to be distracted by fripperies such as the Seven Deadly Sins. The way Marlowe has structured the play means that we know that Faustus will fall, so our focus is upon his thought processes, rather than the outcome. This pattern of repeated moral choices to pursue his chosen course suggests that Faustus brings about his own undoing.

For all his academic brilliance, Faustus appears blind to how he is manipulated and fails to realise that his power isn't quite as it appears. He assumes that his magical capabilities brought Mephistopheles to him, yet Mephistopheles tells him that his conjuring merely attracted him to Faustus. His desire for a wife isn't satisfied. Instead, he is promised courtesans (prostitutes). Along with these warning signs, he also ignores the supernatural appearance of *'Homo fuge'* on his arm and, most tellingly of all, he arrogantly dismisses Mephistopheles's description of the torment of hell. Faustus appears to think he has command of a devil.

Key quotations

How pliant is this Mephistopheles
(Faustus, Act I Scene III)

when we hear one rack the name of God... We fly in hope to get his glorious soul
(Mephistopheles, Act I Scene III)

The middle section of the play sees Faustus use his power, but for superficial ends. He does get to see the world but also spends his time performing conjuring tricks. You might find it instructive to compare his original aims as expressed in Act I Scene I with what he actually achieves in Acts III and IV.

Ironically, you might agree that, in the middle of the play, Marlowe encourages you to side with the light-hearted trickster that Faustus becomes – his playfulness engenders the audience's support and, in many ways, the sequence of the play sees the audience waver in their view of Faustus.

Activity 4

In the middle of the farcical antics of Act IV Scene I, Faustus has a moment to reflect on his fate. Look again at the lines from **'What art thou, Faustus...'** to **'... quiet in conceit'**. and consider these questions.

a) To what extent is Faustus aware of his unfolding tragedy?

b) What are his feelings towards Christ at this point?

c) What is the effect of placing this soliloquy in the middle of the comic mayhem?

The final sequence of Faustus's narrative trajectory sees his demise, yet even when he has opportunities to repent he refuses them, and once again Marlowe invites the audience to judge Faustus. The dialogue with the Old Man in Act V Scene I is revealing: Faustus immediately assumes that he can't be saved. Here we see Faustus in the grip of despair – which in a religious context means a complete loss of faith in the mercy of God.

During the course of the play, we are shown how Faustus becomes isolated from other humans. Valdes and Cornelius disappear from the narrative, his interactions with others are characterised by trickery rather than friendship, and his cruel instruction to Mephistopheles to torture the Old Man confirms his emotional detachment from others. Finally, his separation from God signifies that he is lost. For some readers, the moment where Faustus damns himself is when he kisses Helen, for the sin of demoniality (sexual interaction with spirits) leads the Old Man to state that Faustus is no longer in a position to be saved. In Christian belief, once a person had intercourse with spirits they were damned and had no chance of salvation.

> **Key quotations**
>
> **Damned art thou, Faustus, damned! Despair and die!**
> *(Faustus, Act V Scene I)*
>
> **Torment, sweet friend, that base and crooked age**
> *(Faustus, Act V Scene I)*
>
> **thy soul exclud'st the grace of heaven**
> *(Old Man, Act V Scene I)*

Like most tragic characters, the final scene of Faustus's life sees the protagonist acutely aware of his fate. In a later chapter, you will explore the language of the final soliloquy, but for now consider how Marlowe manipulates your sympathy for Faustus and whether you agree with Faustus's own grasp of the reasons for his downfall.

Activity 5

Look closely at Faustus's soliloquy in Act V Scene II from **'Now hast thou...'** to the end. Consider the questions below.

a) Which lines capture the fear and horror the character feels?

b) What does Faustus ascribe his downfall to?

c) How far do you agree with Faustus's own assessment of his situation?

d) What might his final words **'Ah, Mephistopheles'** mean?

e) What degree of sympathy (or otherwise) do you feel for Faustus at this point in the narrative?

You may have conflicting opinions about the central character, feeling that he is both admirable and foolish. Such a view is not uncommon. In tragic texts, we are invited to see both the shortcomings and heroic qualities of tragic protagonists, so rather than having to firmly decide on one view of Faustus, it may be that you acknowledge the conflicted nature of the character and also your conflicting views. Nonetheless, some readers have strong opinions on the protagonist's actions and you should be prepared to interact with them. The following activities may help shape your own response.

Activity 6

Find evidence from the text to support the following descriptions of Faustus.

- talented
- greedy
- intelligent
- ignorant
- ambitious
- reckless
- selfish
- curious
- hedonistic
- fearful
- regretful
- foolish
- careless
- courageous
- arrogant

Activity 7

Which aspects of the following statements do you feel are accurate? Which sentences do you find it harder to agree with?

> Marlowe presents Faustus as a fool whose practical abilities and academic intelligence lead him to assume arrogantly that the world is his oyster. He fails to read the warning signs because he thinks he knows best. Even his stated intentions are a sham: he wastes his powers and, in doing so, reveals himself to be a shallow individual. At best, he is an entertaining charlatan; at worst, he is cruel. Even when death is near, he still can't see the reasons for his own downfall. His death elicits little sympathy.

> Marlowe encourages the audience to see Faustus as a flawed but interesting character whose verve, enthusiasm and intelligence make him attractive. The world is too narrow for his brilliance and his tragedy is one of situation – he is confined by the limits of religion. His errors are entirely human ones: the inability to see oneself as we truly are is recognisable to the whole audience, and the desire for power and knowledge is common to us in the 21st century. He dies a flawed hero.

Mephistopheles

Marlowe's representation of a devilish figure on stage is much more than the straightforward tempter figure of morality plays. Mephistopheles can be read in a variety of ways and, as with Faustus, the audience can find themselves with conflicting responses to his actions. On one hand, he is clearly trying to damn Faustus and yet he is also presented as a companion figure and a character who might be said to have tragic potential.

The first appearance of Mephistopheles in Act I Scene III is as a devil, the sight of which is **'too ugly'** for Faustus, who makes him reappear as a Franciscan friar. From the start, then, Mephistopheles is not what he appears – or at least he isn't as he appears to Faustus. Yet in many ways, Mephistopheles is truthful: he bluntly tells Faustus that he only obeys Lucifer and arrives in Faustus's study **'in hope to get his glorious soul'** *(Act I, Scene III)*. The first glimpse of the complexity of the character occurs later in Act I Scene III when Mephistopheles explains his relationship with Lucifer and implores Faustus not to follow through with his fatal decision.

Key quotations

… I, who saw the face of God
And tasted the eternal joys of heaven *(Mephistopheles, Act I Scene III)*

… deprived of everlasting bliss *(Mephistopheles, Act I Scene III)*

Activity 8

Read the dialogue between Faustus and Mephistopheles in Act I Scene III from **'Was not that Lucifer...'** to **'... a terror to my fainting soul!'** Answer the following questions.

a) How does Mephistopheles describe Lucifer's fall from heaven and its connection with Faustus?

b) What does the negative manner in which Mephistopheles describes his existence suggest?

c) What does the passionate nature of his advice to Faustus suggest?

d) How do you react to Mephistopheles in this part of the scene? Do you pity him? Explain your ideas.

Mephistopheles's honesty continues when he explains that Lucifer wants Faustus's soul to **'Enlarge his kingdom'** *(Act II Scene I)* and that his joy is finding others to share in his misery. Yet Marlowe also shows us how Mephistopheles is manipulative: when Faustus's blood congeals, he brings fire and in an aside exclaims how he will do anything to ensnare Faustus. When Faustus wavers, it is Mephistopheles who distracts him.

The use of asides encourages the audience to see that Mephistopheles is (at least in part) playing a role for Faustus. This complicates the audience's response as we may now wonder whether Mephistopheles's seemingly heartfelt address to Faustus in Act I Scene III was part of a strategy – some sort of subtle manipulation to win the Doctor's trust.

If you take the view that Mephistopheles is a deceiver and a trickster, plenty of textual evidence supports this. He distracts Faustus with devils and rich apparel in Act II Scene I. He is unable to provide the Doctor with a wife so offers him courtesans and distracts him with a comic devil dressed as a wife. He also gives him books and information about the cosmos. However, it is also worth exploring whether Faustus recognises Mephistopheles's limitations.

Activity 9

Is Faustus being deceived and, if so, is he aware of it? How honest and knowledgeable is Mephistopheles? Read the following segments of the play as starting points for your thinking:

- Act II Scene I from **'How, a wife?...'** to the end

- Act II Scene III from **'When I behold the heavens...'** to '... **renounce this magic and repent'**.

Key quotations

[aside] O, what will not I do to obtain his soul?
(Mephistopheles, Act II Scene I)

[aside] I'll fetch him somewhat to delight his mind.
(Mephistopheles, Act II Scene I)

... marriage is but a ceremonial toy
(Mephistopheles, Act II Scene I)

Some readers note the close relationship between Mephistopheles and Faustus that develops during the play. Remember that the action of the narrative spans 24 years, so in the middle acts we see more of the companionship of the two characters, to the point where they seem to be almost a double act. This closeness is reflected in the terms of address such as 'Sweet Mephistopheles', 'gentle Mephistopheles' and 'my Faustus'. Faustus in particular extends his affection at times, and often in performance the energy of the two characters in the farcical scenes suggests a lively, intimate friendship in which the duo enjoy their trickery together.

Oliver Ryan as Faustus and Sandy Grierson as Mephistopheles in the RSC production, 2016

Activity 10

Look closely at Act III Scene I from '**Having now, my good Mephistopheles...**' to '**... thou shalt not be discerned**', noting the way in which Mephistopheles and Faustus interact. In particular, explore the questions below.

a) Which character appears to hold more power? Who, if anyone, is in charge?

b) Consider the energy and patterns of language shared by the two characters. Do they appear to speak in similar ways here?

c) Explore the on-stage interaction between them. How do you picture this in performance? If you directed this scene, how would you advise the actors with regard to body language?

Much of the trickery in Act III relies on the two characters working together. Mephistopheles happily follows Faustus's instructions when they tease the Pope. The audience see a playful Mephistopheles, yet in Act III Scene II he appears vexed and angry when he chides Robin and the Vintner.

As part of the contract, he has agreed to assist Faustus and he appears to do so willingly. When instructed to remove the horns from the Knight in Act IV Scene I, he does so promptly. When trying to impress the Duchess of Vanholt in Act IV Scene II, Faustus abruptly orders his partner to acquire grapes, saying **'Mephistopheles, begone!'** and the instruction is carried out without complaint. A similar act occurs in Act V Scene I when Mephistopheles conjures the spirit of Helen of Greece. In Act V Scene I, Marlowe presents Mephistopheles in a much more sinister light. The appearance of the Old Man is a climactic point because Faustus is on the brink of salvation and at this point Mephistopheles invites the Doctor to commit suicide by presenting him with a dagger. For some Christians, such an act was regarded as a sin because only God had the right to decide when a person's life ended. When this doesn't work, Mephistopheles threatens to tear Faustus to pieces and it seems that the power structures in the world of the text are exposed.

Activity 11

The stage directions in Act V Scene I reveal much about Mephistopheles's conduct. What are the implications of the following directions?

- *Music sounds and Helen, [led in by Mephistopheles,] passeth over the stage*
- *Mephistopheles gives him a dagger*

Activity 12

Read the dialogue in Act V Scene I from **'Torment, sweet friend...'** to **'... which is but little worth'**, which reveal both the extent and the limits of Mephistopheles's power. In terms of the three characters connected to these lines (Faustus, Mephistopheles and the Old Man), who has the most power and why?

Following the threat, a more fawning Mephistopheles presents Helen, presumably because he knows this will clinch Faustus's damnation. As the play draws to a close, a critical moment in the relationship between the two main characters emerges when Mephistopheles advises Faustus of **'greater danger'** and threatens him should he fail to follow through on his deal with Lucifer *(Act V Scene I)*. His final lines to Faustus offer no comfort. For some audiences, Mephistopheles is an arch-deceiver whose actions are all simply an act. From the outset, he is a character who tricks Faustus and therefore it is difficult to have any sympathy with his position. Viewed this way, Mephistopheles fulfils the role of antagonist – a tragic villain whose actions bring about the downfall of the protagonist.

Yet it is possible to view Mephistopheles as a tragic character, one whose position may elicit some understanding, if not sympathy. He is very much like Adam, Icarus, Lucifer and Faustus in that his torment is wrought by his own ambition.

Activity 13

Look again at Act V Scene I from **'Thou traitor, Faustus...'** to **'... do attend thy drift'**. There are various ways the actor playing Mephistopheles might deliver these lines, which would alter the meaning of them. Do you see these lines as vindictive or desperate?

Activity 14

Now explore the whole of Act V Scene I. Does this scene prove that Mephistopheles is nothing more than a deeply deceptive, sinister antagonist?

Activity 15

The list below is a reminder of the conventional features of a tragic character. Does Mephistopheles exhibit any of these characteristics? Is it too much of a leap to say that Mephistopheles is tragic?

- Tragic characters suffer during most of the play and reluctantly see that their way of life or their choices were wrong. In spite of this, they proceed with a sense of noble futility

- Tragic characters are destroyed by their own mistakes or some flaw in their character. They are also victims of tragic villains or fate, or both

- Tragic characters provoke negative responses in the audience. Their actions cause revulsion and their arrogance can be an unattractive quality

- Tragic characters provoke positive responses in the audience. Their self-belief and grandeur can be heroic, their philosophical manner attractive and the scale of their suffering a cause for sympathy.

Chorus

The Chorus fulfils a range of functions in the play. On a practical level, some of the aspects of Faustus's travels are impossible to recreate on stage, so the Chorus's account of these events sidesteps these problems, while filling in parts of the story for the audience. It's also the case that when time-shifts occur in the narrative, the Chorus outlines some of the details not represented in the 24-year span of the action.

In performance, the role is performed by a single actor rather than a group of actors, as was the case in older Greek drama. In terms of the content of the Chorus's lines, you noticed earlier how in the Prologue the Chorus offers the audience an initial view of Faustus, which in places casts him in an unfavourable light. The words of the Chorus elsewhere seem to adopt a less judgmental stance towards Faustus.

The fourth and final appearance of the Chorus is in the Epilogue following the demise of Faustus. As the closing words in the play, they appear to function as the closing moral – words of advice to the audience that sum up the lessons learned. There is an elevated quality, with references to the laurel (the leaf of which was seen as an emblem of poetic achievement) and Apollo, the god of learning. The play ends with a reminder to the wise to remember their limits.

Activity 16

Do you agree with the view that 'the Act III Chorus and Act IV Chorus seem to be celebrating Faustus's achievements'? Find words and phrases from these parts of the text that convey a sense of enthusiasm and energy.

Activity 17

Which, if either, of these opinions reflect your reading of the Epilogue?

> The words of the Chorus present Faustus in reverential tones: the references to Apollo and the laurel ally him with respectable images. His educational prowess and potential greatness is celebrated. The sense that some good comes from his demise emerges: the Chorus sadly acknowledges his fall and the play ends on a sombre note.

> The Epilogue seems anticlimactic. It reduces the scope of Faustus's life to a mere few lines. Negative words such as 'cut', 'burned' and 'fall' are central and his story is compressed into three words: **'Faustus is gone'** (Chorus), which seem dismissive. It reads as a finger-wagging warning to the audience that they should remember that God is the boss.

Old Man

The naming of this character should alert you that he is an archetype rather than a fully realised role. He does represent the force of good in the play and reminds the audience that choice is still possible and that God's mercy is stronger than Lucifer's control. Unlike the Good Angel, who seems to be an externalisation of Faustus's psyche (the human mind, soul or spirit), the Old Man appears to be 'real' and interacts with Faustus. Often in literature, a protagonist will have a mentor figure, an older character whose age signifies wisdom. Crucially, Faustus rejects the Old Man's advice and instructs Mephistopheles to torture him, which serves to emphasise the cruelty to which Faustus has stooped.

The Old Man's contribution to the play is minimal, but he is introduced into the narrative at a crucial point, appearing just after Helen enters. One of his actions is to save Faustus from suicide, yet when he re-enters later in Act V Scene I, he also expresses the hopelessness of Faustus's situation.

He offers Faustus a final chance of redemption, the rejection of which reveals that the Doctor has made his choice. The Old Man noticeably differs between the A text and B text, so it is worth considering the varying emphases Marlowe gives this character in the two versions.

Activity 18

Read the following extracts from the Old Man's speech in Act V Scene I from the A text and B text. Consider:

- the harassing tone of the A text and the conciliatory tone of the B text
- the negative word choices of the A text and the positive ones in the B text
- the manner in which Faustus is addressed in both versions.

> **A text**
>
> Break heart, drop blood, and mingle it with tears –
> Tears falling from repentant heaviness
> Of thy most vile and loathsome filthiness,
> The stench whereof corrupts the inward soul
> With such flagitious crimes of heinous sins
> As no commiseration may expel
> But mercy, Faustus, of thy Saviour sweet,
> Whose blood alone must wash away thy guilt. *(Old Man, Act V Scene I)*

> **B text**
>
> It may be, this my exhortation
> Seems harsh and all unpleasant: let it not;
> For, gentle son, I speak it not in wrath,
> Or envy of thee, but in tender love
> And pity of thy future misery;
> And so have hope that this my kind rebuke,
> Checking thy body, may amend thy soul. *(Old Man, Act V Scene I)*

You will have noticed that the B text version presents the Old Man as a friendly advisor. There is a paternal quality to the words and this perhaps explains why Faustus takes note and seems on the verge of repentance. His subsequent instruction to Mephistopheles to torture the Old Man also seems much harsher. Some readers see the Old Man as a version of Christ. However you choose to interpret this character, the actions of this part of the play seem to echo a central motif in the text: the rejection of a father figure.

The Good and Evil Angels

So far you have interpreted the Good and Evil Angels as representing the conflict within Faustus's soul. Their first appearance in Act I Scene I certainly has the quality of psychomachia (the literary representation of a conflict in the mind or soul; taken from the title of a work by 5th-century poet, Prudentius) and acts like soliloquy, giving voice to the protagonist's thoughts. Yet dramatically, they seem to break the mood of the scene in which Faustus's soliloquy invites the audience into his confidence. The Good Angel's words are the only indication so far that the Doctor has any doubts – externally he seems to have little doubt about his situation.

However, it is possible to see these characters as something more than an externalisation of Faustus's feelings. If you read them as representatives of a wider cosmological context (in the same way as Lucifer and the demons), then their appearance in Act I Scene I serves as a reminder that there are other factors beyond the narrow individual world of Faustus in his study. Their appearance alerts the audience to the idea that other entities and theological forces are operating in a way that Faustus ignores.

The oppositional words of the Angels in Act II Scene I occur at a point where Faustus is wavering. Marlowe has Faustus echo the final word of the Evil Angel – **'wealth'** – and whether he begins to hear the Angels or not is debatable. The suggestion is that his view of the world is closer to that of the Evil Angel. In the Context chapter, you explored the different views of salvation and predestination, and so a further way of interpreting the Angels is as representative of two concepts of human fate. The Good Angel suggests that individuals have the ability to choose to be saved. The Evil Angel and Faustus appear to believe that fate is determined and Faustus is damned anyway. By the final act, Faustus can hear the words of the Evil Angel, signifying that he has accepted the fate awaiting him.

Activity 19

How do you, as a 21st-century reader, react to the use of the Good and Evil Angels? Which of the following views is closest to your own?

> They are integral to the themes and issues of the play and have symbolic significance.

> They are oddly cartoonish additions that add drama to the play, but add little in terms of meaning.

Key quotation

GOOD ANGEL: Sweet Faustus, think of heaven and heavenly things.

EVIL ANGEL: No, Faustus, think of honour and wealth. *(Act II Scene I)*

Helen of Greece (known as Helen of Troy)

The dramatic moment when Faustus kisses Helen of Greece seals his fate. The characters are well aware that Helen is an infernal illusion, but they ignore this truth and admire her superficial appearance. In spite of his warning to the Emperor about touching Darius and Alexander, Faustus has contact with Helen, ironically asking to be made immortal. In Greek myth, Helen of Greece was taken by Paris after he was promised her by the goddess Aphrodite. Her husband, Menelaus, regained her following the ten-year Trojan War. Faustus's famous description of her as 'the face that launched a thousand ships' acknowledges both her beauty and the destruction that male competition for her brought. It is the Scholars, men who supposedly should be more logical, who first request Faustus to conjure Helen.

Key quotations

... the pride of nature's works
And only paragon of excellence
(First Scholar, Act V Scene I)

Her lips sucks forth my soul
(Faustus, Act V Scene I)

Helen of Troy is certainly not what she seems in this 2010 Royal Exchange Theatre production

Which, if either, of the following seem plausible reasons why Faustus kisses Helen?

> Much like the Seven Deadly Sins, he uses her as a distraction from his awareness that he is doomed.

> Faustus consciously kisses her to put an end to his wavering – he knows that after this act he is damned.

Wagner

Wagner is a loyal and respectful servant to Faustus, one who will benefit from Faustus's will. On occasion, he has the function of commentator, such as in Act V Scene I where he wonders why Faustus holds a banquet when his death is at hand. He also serves as a mechanism to name and introduce characters for the benefit of the audience, as seen in Act IV Scene I where he tells Faustus of the Duke of Vanholt's request. In the A text, Wagner performs the Chorus speech for Act III; in many stage versions of the play, he is given some or all of the Chorus's speech.

Wagner can be seen in the comedic tradition of the clever servant who upstages his supposed betters. This is seen in Act I Scene II where he teases the Scholars and parodies the language of logic and religion. The main significance of Wagner is to illuminate the master–servant motif. After Faustus has acquired the services of Mephistopheles, Wagner exerts his power over Robin in Act I Scene IV, a hilarious parody of the main plot. Marlowe alerts the audience to the manner in which power operates and undermines the serious aspects of the Faustus story, most notably when it emerges that Wagner, a mere servant, can perform magic too. By using Wagner as a structural parallel to Faustus, the foolishness of Faustus is reinforced.

Actors perform on a giant clock face at the Staatsoper Unter den Linden theatre, Berlin, in the 2006 opera *Faustus, The Last Night*, based on Marlowe's play

Minor characters

Several characters in the play have less significant roles and are mainly of interest because of Faustus's interactions with them or their structural role. You will explore the depiction of the Pope in the Themes chapter and the comic characters in the Performance chapter.

Activity 21

Consider how Marlowe uses some of the minor characters.

a) Explore the function of Valdes and Cornelius in Act I Scene I. They encourage and instruct Faustus, but is their role any more than a version of the tempter figure in the morality play?

b) Consider the differences in the role and attitudes the Scholars present towards Faustus in Act I Scene II and then in Act V Scene II. Is there any sense in which the values they stand for are satirised?

c) Explore the function of the characters such as the Pope, the Emperor, and the Duke and Duchess of Vanholt. What effect is created by the way in which powerful characters regard Faustus?

d) Look again at the actions and role of Robin in Act I Scene IV and Act II Scene II. What differences do you notice in terms of his power in these scenes? Is he anything more than a comic character?

Writing about character

Thinking about characters in relation to their functions in the narrative will help you to see the way in which their stories contribute to the design of the play as a whole. Be alert for parallels between characters, especially the way in which the actions and words of characters are echoed by another. Look carefully at how characters appear to be archetypes, but also how the playwright gives them complexity, making them rounded rather than one-dimensional.

Try to write about characters in relation to dramatic method. Explore, for example, who is given soliloquies and asides, and at which points in the narrative. Think about the journeys of characters in the story and where each character ends up. Consider which characters gain the audience's sympathies and why. Which actions invite you to understand their suffering? Are you, as the audience, in possession of more information about the characters than they are? Draw together these elements and then conclude how they function within the play.

Doctor Faustus is a play of many elements, blending religion, the supernatural, tragedy, farce and the morality play. The language in the text is therefore varied, containing **lyrical** soliloquy alongside hilarious comic prose. In this chapter, you will look at some of these patterns of language across the play and explore some specific scenes too. Close analysis of language is most useful when it is related to the wider ideas and characterisation of a text.

Use the following analysis of the Prologue as a starting point for your study and to see which aspects of language are most productive to explore. Then use Activity 1 on page 62 to link language features to wider meanings.

Analysing language: an example

Remind yourself of the Prologue printed below then read the commentary that follows.

Enter Chorus

CHORUS   Not marching now in fields of Trasimene
Where Mars did mate the Carthaginians,
Nor sporting in the dalliance of love
In courts of kings where state is overturned,
Nor in the pomp of proud audacious deeds,   5
Intends our muse to daunt his heavenly verse.
Only this, gentlemen: we must perform
The form of Faustus' fortunes, good or bad.
To patient judgements we appeal our plaud,
And speak for Faustus in his infancy.   10
Now is he born, his parents base of stock,
In Germany, within a town called Rhode.
Of riper years to Wittenberg he went,
Whereas his kinsmen chiefly brought him up.
So soon he profits in divinity,   15
The fruitful plot of scholarism graced,
That shortly he was graced with doctor's name,
Excelling all whose sweet delight disputes
In heavenly matters of theology;
Till, swoll'n with cunning of a self-conceit,   20
His waxen wings did mount above his reach,
And melting heavens conspired his overthrow.

For, falling to a devilish exercise,
And glutted more with learning's golden gifts,
He surfeits upon cursed necromancy;   25
Nothing so sweet as magic is to him,
Which he prefers before his chiefest bliss.
And this the man that in his study sits.

Exit

(Chorus, Prologue)

Commentary

The overall shape of the Prologue moves the audience from grandiose, sweeping **imagery** of myth, battle and state to the enclosed, private world of Faustus's study. There is a **rhetorical** flourish to the opening lines, which tells what the tale is *not* about, before revealing the general direction of the story that follows. The language has an elevated feel, in part because of the references to the Roman god Mars and the Punic wars (Trasimene was a battle in the wars fought by the Carthaginians), and partly because of the relative complexity of **polysyllabic** words such as 'dalliance' and 'audacious'. The lyrical qualities of the first six lines are aided by the use of **iambic pentameter**, which alerts the audience to the relative seriousness of the piece.

The reference to **'our muse'** also has a **metafictional** feel: it seems the speaker is stepping out of the story for a moment (with the 'our' perhaps referring to the company of actors) and slightly distancing the playwright from the content – as if the **muse** of inspiration has compelled Marlowe to present the story. The elevated feel is broken in line 7 (**'Only this, gentlemen'**), which disrupts the rhythm and signifies a shift in the narrative focus to Faustus. The **modal verb** 'must' gives a feel of urgency to the story, as does the shift into present tense with **'Now is he born'**. The effect is one of immediacy, as if the audience is invited to picture the moment of the scene.

iambic pentameter a line of ten syllables consisting of five unstressed and five stressed syllables

imagery the use of visual or other sensual references

lyrical having an emotional and imaginative quality

metafictional referring to narratives that draw attention to their artifice; parts of stories that acknowledge their literary qualities

modal verb a type of verb conveying intent or possibility, e.g. must, may, will, should, etc.

muse a source of inspiration; in Greek mythology, the Muses were nine goddesses who presided over the arts and sciences

polysyllabic referring to words with several syllables

rhetorical referring to speech or text intended to influence or persuade

There is a playful quality to some word choices – Marlowe exploits the double meaning of **'heavenly'**, which means both 'delightful' and 'of God'. Likewise, the use of words associated with nature and taste such as **'riper'**, **'fruitful'** and **'sweet'** have echoes of the Adam story. There is an irony to the line **'sweet delight disputes'**, whereby the product of Faustus's dispute with theology is anything but sweet. Words connected with greed such as **'swoll'n'**, **'glutted'** and **'surfeits'** towards the end of the speech paint Faustus in a less attractive way, and the double meaning on **'falling'**, which literally means 'getting on with' but also refers to Icarus's descent and, by extension, Faustus's tragedy.

Activity 1

Having read the commentary, which of the following statements do you think best captures the effect of the language in the Prologue?

> The language elevates the story of Faustus, suggesting it is worth our attention. By using culturally significant references and stately rhythms, the Prologue invites the audience to see Faustus as a serious tragic protagonist.

> The language is elevated in an ironic way – it's so over the top and playful that the audience see that the Prologue undercuts Faustus: amid all the important references, he's just a greedy, selfish little man in his study.

Tips for assessment

The religious references are an important part of *Doctor Faustus*. You can comment on specific words and phrases to explore how Marlowe reflects the religious context in which the play was written – but remember to tie them to the wider meanings of the play. For instance, you could explore how religious references in Act III Scene I are used for the purposes of comedy.

Kit Harrington's Faustus enjoys sweet delights in a 2016 production

The energy of Marlowe's verse

Marlowe's verse has a muscular quality, in part coming from the regularity of the **blank verse** he employs, which provides a sense of driving rhythm at times, but also the way he manipulates this form by varying stresses and rhythms to suit the action. For instance, Faustus's speech in Act I Scene I beginning **'How am I glutted…'** is written in iambic pentameter throughout and has an intensity that reflects the feverous excitement of the protagonist. Coupled with the range of geographical and political references, the repetition of the pronoun 'I' and the **alliteration** of words such as 'pleasant' and 'princely', the effect is one of verve, strength and egotism.

You may have noticed the alternation between **monosyllabic** and polysyllabic words. Although there are some reasonably complex words such as 'philosophy' and 'servile', many of the words in this speech are monosyllabic; they have a directness that fits with the mood of the protagonist. **'I'll have them fly to India for gold'** is a good example of the straightforward, largely monosyllabic nature of the speech (*Act I Scene I*).

Yet there are times when the rhythm isn't quite so steady. At the start of Act II Scene I, Faustus reflects on his situation and the uncertainty of his thinking appears to be reflected in the natural pauses in the pentameter. The opening line **'Now, Faustus, must thou needs be damned'** invites pauses where the comma falls. Perhaps the stress falls on the first syllable rather than the second.

At times of importance, reversing the stress on the syllables can alert the audience to a significant event in the play. For example, in Act I Scene III when Faustus instructs Mephistopheles to seek Lucifer's approval for the contract, the pattern is **trochaic**, with the stress falling on the word 'Go' rather than 'and' in **'Go and return to mighty Lucifer'**. Of course, an actor's delivery of these lines is never as stilted as these rhythms might suggest, but the loose pulse of them can be felt and, in the above case, the emphasis given to the imperative 'Go' suggests that the action is significant, as indeed it is: here, Faustus takes a big step towards damnation.

---

alliteration the repetition of consonant sounds at the start of words

blank verse unrhymed lines of iambic pentameter

monosyllabic referring to words of one syllable

trochaic referring to a rhythm that inverts the iambic stress, i.e. a stressed syllable followed by an unstressed syllable

---

Activity 2

Practise your ability to analyse the language of Marlowe's verse closely. Write an analysis of Faustus's speech in Act I Scene III from **'Had I as many souls…'** to the end, considering the effect of images and references, rhythm, alliteration and syllable counts. Remember to link your observations to meanings and ideas.

Elevated language

You will have noticed that tragic language is lofty and artfully shaped; the characters offer their thoughts in **elevated language**. Tragic plays often treat their subject matter in a philosophical way, rendering excruciating experiences in an artistic manner. It's highly unlikely, for instance, that a person facing death in real life would be able to utter a skilfully constructed speech that captures the essence of the human condition (as Faustus does in Act V Scene II). But tragedies are art, not real life, so listening to the carefully crafted ways in which awful events are relayed is part of the joy of *Doctor Faustus.*

In a play dealing with spiritual issues, it's no surprise that the concepts themselves are rendered in complex, elevated terms. There are times when it seems the base nature of Faustus's actions is dressed up in fanciful words. For instance, in Cornelius's speech in Act I Scene I, in which he extols the virtues of magic, the references include miracles, astrology, spirits and forefathers. There is a bombastic (pompous) quality to the speech, which presents the benefits of necromancy in glowing terms.

Activity 3

Read the Chorus's speech that appears before Act III. Make a list of all the elevated words and concepts referred to. What effect is created?

The most recognisable speech in the play occurs when Faustus describes Helen's beauty in Act V Scene I. It is a speech that exemplifies the lofty and lyrical beauty of the best of Marlowe's verse. The tragic qualities are evident from the link with Greek myth, where Helen's beauty (her face) is the wellspring of conflict. There is a grandeur to the play's most famous lines: **'Was this the face that launched a thousand ships / And burnt the topless towers of Ilium?'** *(Faustus, Act V Scene I).*

Helen becomes a **metaphor** for Faustus's situation: like Troy, he too will be destroyed by an image. The destruction of Troy happens because of the outward appearance of Helen. The destruction of Faustus happens because he is seduced by an illusion. The speech itself is laden with aggressive verbs such as 'sacked', 'combat' and 'wound'. It uses **hyperbole** to emphasise Helen's beauty: she is **'fairer than the evening air'**, brighter **'than flaming Jupiter'** and **'More lovely than the monarch of the sky'** *(Faustus, Act V Scene I).*

There is horrible irony here in that Faustus (and possibly the audience) seems spellbound by the beauty of the words, but of course Helen is a trap: kissing her seals Faustus's fate. The hyperbole belies the destruction she brings.

Activity 4

In Act V Scene I, Faustus proclaims **'Her lips sucks forth my soul. See where it flies!'** What do you notice about the complexity of the words in comparison to the rest of the speech? What might be said about the **caesura** in the middle of the line?

caesura a break or pause in a line of verse

elevated language words that rise above the ordinary, often in beautifully poetic ways

hyperbole deliberately exaggerated phrases

metaphor a figure of speech describing a person or thing by comparing them with something that is not literally applicable

Activity 5

How do you interpret the metaphorical use of Helen? Consider the following four views. Which, if any, do you agree with?

> Faustus sees Helen as a representation of his own obsession with necromancy: both appear seductive but bring destruction.

> Faustus sees Helen as a version of Mephistopheles. She isn't as she appears, and neither is Mephistopheles. Helen is a metaphor of Faustus's victimhood.

> Helen symbolises the folly of humanity in its inability to avoid temptation, even though the dangers are obvious.

> Helen is a tragic symbol of how humanity causes its own destruction: Faustus conjures her, and his own doom results.

Elizabeth Taylor as Helen and Richard Burton as Faustus in the 1967 film

Irony and polysemy: the danger of words

Some of the ironies in the play are more to do with situation than language, such as the idea that the great logician Faustus exchanges his soul for some books, or that his servant can perform the sort of tricks that Faustus can, without jeopardising his salvation. Yet linguistic irony is central to Faustus's plight.

As you noticed in the analysis of Helen, there is a significant irony in that she appears attractive but brings destruction. Faustus can't be unaware of the danger, yet he proceeds. His own hyperbolic description of her charms seems to persuade him, almost as if language itself becomes a sort of illusion. The further irony is of course that earlier in Act V Scene II Faustus says he wishes he had **'never read book'**.

Here we see a man who on a surface level acknowledges the danger of words, then falls victim to his own fanciful descriptions. The powerful words of Cornelius in Act I Scene I have a similar effect, dangling the promise of power and majesty while obscuring the dangers of necromancy. The play indicates that part of Faustus's tragedy is his willingness to look beyond the obvious pitfalls of his actions, while allowing himself to get swept along on the power of language.

Some of the words in the play are **polysemic**; their ambiguity shines a light on the irony of the situation. For instance, in Act I Scene I, Faustus proclaims **'necromantic books are heavenly'**. From Faustus's perspective, he means something like 'inspirational' or 'uplifting', but the audience see the ambiguity of the word 'heavenly', which also refers to God. Clearly the books can't be a product of God's heaven – quite the reverse – and so the irony of this line provokes a grim humour. It signals that Faustus is so caught up in his words and actions that he fails to see the trap. For the audience, this is a dramatic irony, echoing the asides of Mephistopheles in Act II Scene I where we see a wider perspective than Faustus does.

> **polysemy** the existence of more than one meaning for words

Activity 6

Consider the polysemic nature of the following words. What different meanings do they have and what might they reveal about situation and character?

a) 'conspired' in **'heavens conspired his overthrow'** *(Chorus, Prologue)*

b) 'falling' in **'falling to a devilish exercise'** *(Chorus, Prologue)*

c) 'virtue' in **'there's virtue in my heavenly words'** *(Faustus, Act I Scene III)*

d) 'confounds' in **'confounds hell in Elysium'** *(Faustus, Act I Scene III)*

Symbolism and imagery

Literary texts make use of symbols and images to illuminate themes and central ideas. As you've already seen in Activity 5, Helen can be read as a symbol in numerous ways.

Blood

References to blood are made throughout the text and they acquire a symbolic resonance. Blood not only refers to the physical liquid emanating from Faustus's arm, but also has a religious significance. In Christian teachings, the blood of Christ is a symbol for resurrection – when Christ's blood is shed on the cross, it's a symbol of his sacrifice for humanity: in giving up his life, humans can have an everlasting life in heaven. In Act II Scene I, where Faustus makes his deal with Lucifer, blood is referred to many times, as listed below.

> **Key quotations**
>
> To him I'll build an altar and a church,
> And offer lukewarm blood of new-born babes.
> *(Faustus, Act II Scene I)*
>
> And write a deed of gift with thine own blood,
> For that security craves great Lucifer.
> *(Mephistopheles, Act II Scene I)*
>
> I cut mine arm, and with my proper blood
> Assure my soul to be great Lucifer's
> *(Faustus, Act II Scene I)*
>
> My blood congeals, and I can write no more.
> *(Faustus, Act II Scene I)*
>
> What might the staying of my blood portend?
> *(Faustus, Act II Scene I)*
>
> So. Now the blood begins to clear again.
> Now will I make an end immediately.
> *(Faustus, Act II Scene I)*

In the first example, you can see how Faustus commits blasphemy by appropriating the features of a Christian church and using them to offer a blood sacrifice to Lucifer. There is an echo of the Last Supper here, the event in the Bible where Jesus has a final meal with the disciples and offers them wine, telling them it represents his blood. This act is commemorated in the Christian sacrament of the Eucharist, where bread and wine are taken as symbols of Christ's body and blood. Given this context, you can see how the reference to blood in Faustus's words holds strikingly sacrilegious connotations.

The Last Supper (1562) by Juan de Juanes

Activity 7

Explore the remaining blood references in the list on page 67. What added meanings beyond the literal can you find in these quotations?

Activity 8

Now consider the ideas associated with blood in Act V Scene II. Start with **'See, see where Christ's blood streams in the firmament!'**

Nature

Images connected with nature are often assumed to be positive: humans have a tendency to ascribe sentimental, pastoral qualities to nature. Images of Mother Nature as fertile and bountiful are familiar ones, and in some texts, Nature is presented as truthful, wise and ungoverned by man's corruption. However, you only need to consider the symbolism of the snake in the Garden of Eden to see that how we read natural imagery depends very much upon the context in which it is used.

You have already seen how the Prologue uses words related to nature such as 'fruitful' and 'riper' to present the positive aspects of Faustus's early life. In the Epilogue, natural images are used for a different purpose: to present his downfall. The images are metaphors based around the destruction of nature. Faustus is compared to a **'branch that might have grown full straight'** *(Chorus, Epilogue)*. You will notice that the first word in this line is 'Cut', with the emphasis placed on the monosyllabic bluntness of this action. The second line, with its reference to **'Apollo's laurel bough'**, is prefaced with the word 'burnèd'. In both cases, the images suggest the destruction of nature. The implication is that Faustus's actions are *un*-natural in the sense that they go against the world and, by extension, God.

Comedic prose

The language of comedy is less elevated than tragedy, often relying on quick-fire dialogue, double meanings and crude puns. There are several scenes of comedy involving Faustus that are written in blank verse, but the scenes featuring the lower characters are written in prose. As you have seen, one of the functions of the comic scenes is to parody the action in the main plot, so when Faustus acquires Mephistopheles, Wagner then attempts to secure the services of Robin. But the comedy also stands on its own as entertainment and, for many audiences, the hilarity of the comic scenes are as memorable as the tragic ones.

The interaction between Wagner and the Scholars in Act I Scene II offers an insight into the way the comedy operates in the play. Lines 1–18 offer rapid interchange between the characters where the meanings of words are played with for comic effect. For instance, in the following segment, you can see how the comic inversion of power creates humour:

> **Key quotation**
>
> | FIRST SCHOLAR: | How now, sirrah, where's thy master? |
> | --- | --- |
> | WAGNER: | God in heaven knows. |
> | SECOND SCHOLAR: | Why, dost not thou know? |
> | WAGNER: | Yes, I know, but that follows not. |
> | FIRST SCHOLAR: | Go to, sirrah! Leave your jesting, and tell us where he is. |
> | WAGNER: | That follows not necessary by force of argument that you, being licentiate, should stand upon't. Therefore, acknowledge your error, and be attentive. |
>
> *(Act I Scene II)*

In terms of social status, the Scholars outrank Wagner, a mere servant. The term of address 'sirrah' is a signifier of this, being a word used when talking to younger people or those with less status. Wagner subverts those hierarchies here by playing the logicians at their own game. Without missing a beat, he responds with the nicely ambiguous phrase '**God in heaven knows**', which on the surface means 'I haven't a clue', but also has a double meaning suggesting that God really does know Faustus's whereabouts – he is conjuring the devil.

Notice how the comedy relies on the audience understanding this pun and being on the same level as Wagner, with the Scholars appearing less aware. Comedy often works in reversing the power structures, suggesting a satirical point – that the powerful in society aren't necessarily the sharpest characters. The comedy is ramped up when Wagner parodies the language of the Scholars, finding holes in their logic and employing complex words and speaking in a multi-clausal sentence, which imitates the language of law and logic.

Activity 10

Read the dialogue between Wagner and Robin in Act I Scene IV. Identify the following comic features of language:

- terms of address
- exclamatory and exaggerated phrases
- elevated language for comic effect
- references to basic matters and beings.

Soliloquy

To some modern dramatists, soliloquy is an archaic device; as a way of revealing the inner thoughts of characters, it seems basic. Having a character voice their views directly to an audience might seem unsubtle, yet many of the finest pieces of poetry are found in literary soliloquy. One of the finest is the last speech of Faustus before he is dragged to hell.

The speech in Act V Scene II is the high point of the play, the moment the drama has been building towards. As the climax of the narrative, it is artfully shaped, beginning with **'Ah, Faustus'** and ending with **'Ah, Mephistopheles'**, as if the individual world of Faustus finally gives way to the wider diabolical forces in the world of the play. As in the rest of the text, time is compressed, with the 59 lines of the soliloquy covering a full hour of 'real' time. The speech is punctuated by the striking of clocks and watches, counting down the time to Faustus's damnation and reminding him of the inevitability of his fate. The effect is one that emphasises the unavoidable nature of tragedy.

The patterns of imagery and the movement in the speech are worthy of exploration. The speech begins with Faustus in imperative mood, attempting to command time to stand still. The temporal imagery includes the spheres, nature, years, days and hours. The stars, the devil and Christ are invoked. Towards the end, the physical nature of the soliloquy comes to the fore, where Faustus is pulled down and sees visions of Christ's blood, Lucifer and then an ireful God. The latter half of the soliloquy contains images of escape.

Activity 11

Look closely at the soliloquy in Act V Scene II.

a) Make a list of the range of imagery in this part of the soliloquy.

b) Make a list of the various means by which Faustus imagines escaping his fate.

It seems that Faustus can see the entities he refers to in his speech; his last words are addressed to God, hell and Lucifer. The final four lines are absolute panic, laden with exclamations and futile imperatives. The final line sees Faustus attempt to offer a deal – **'I'll burn my books'** *(Act V Scene II)* – which even at this late stage perhaps implies that he still hasn't realised that it is himself, rather than his books, that is the cause of his horror.

Activity 12

Faustus's final words – **'Ah, Mephistopheles'** – have an enigmatic quality. Which, if any, of the following statements do you feel sums up their meaning?

> These are the words of an absolutely desperate man. They are shrieked as he looks to Mephistopheles for help, realising that none is forthcoming. The audience feel abject pity for Faustus.

> The words reveal Faustus's ongoing inability to see Mephistopheles for what he is. He speaks them hopefully, expecting some sort of assistance. The audience views Faustus as the deluded man he has been throughout the play.

> These are the words of resignation. With his final breath, Faustus gives in and accepts his fate. He sees Mephistopheles and now accepts his place in hell with a grudging acceptance.

Writing about language

When you write about language, never do it in isolation. You will not say much by simply spotting features. Instead, points about language should be linked closely to ideas about meaning and character. This chapter has focused on the larger features of language such as imagery, symbolism, irony and polysemy, and what they reveal about the ideas in the play. There may be times when exploring the connotations of single words is useful because it illuminates an aspect of character, such as Faustus's final two words. Remember to use words as a springboard to write about what they reveal about character, theme and genre.

Themes – the ideas that recur throughout a story – are a way of unifying a play. For instance, there are many references to religion in *Doctor Faustus*, which is explored through the actions of different characters and scenes. In seeing thematic ideas played and replayed during the course of the play, the audience come to see what they consider to be 'the point' of the story.

Themes often explore moral ideas, concepts that seem applicable to the lives of most people. They invite us to see the text as having a kind of unity of design – an ordered, shaped message that comes to represent what is 'meant' by *Doctor Faustus*. As with character and performance, themes can be interpreted in various ways and can provoke a range of readings.

Mephistopheles appearing to Faustus, from a 1631 edition of the play

Power

At the heart of the play is a story about power. On one level it is a play about masters and servants as played out in both the main plot and the comic scenes. Faustus is a powerful man who wants to know more and be more. The narrative explores what he is prepared to do to get power and how, in doing so, he actually loses it. One reading of the play is that it is a cautionary tale to obey the hierarchical structures that society bequeaths to us; this applies not just to human society, but also to the supernatural worlds of heaven and hell. As a starting point for considering this theme, think about the power balances in the text.

Activity 1

Remind yourself of the events of Act I and try to put the following characters in a rank order from most powerful to least powerful. Which characters and relationships are hardest to decide upon?

- Faustus
- Wagner
- Angels
- Valdes and Cornelius
- Scholars
- Mephistopheles
- Lucifer
- Robin

Activity 2

Now consider the relative power of Faustus, Mephistopheles, Lucifer and God by the end of the text. Where does the power lie and why?

In the Plot and Structure chapter you looked at Faustus's speech in Act I Scene I where he fantasises about what he could do with magical power. Look again at the precise nature of the powers he seeks. Some are connected to the acquisition of riches and delicacies (gold, orient pearl, fruits), some are connected with knowledge (the secrets of foreign kings), some political (chasing the Prince of Parma) and some are altruistic (filling public schools with silk). In order to achieve these and more, an exchange of power has to take place.

Activity 3

Now look closely at Act I Scene III and makes notes on each of the points below.

a) The precise demands Faustus makes in exchange for his soul. Which are selfish and which are altruistic?

b) The manner in which Faustus addresses Mephistopheles, including the use of imperatives. How does Mephistopheles react to Faustus?

c) The things Faustus says he will do with his power. What do these desires reveal about Faustus?

Faustus's desire for power stems from the desire for knowledge, which as you saw in the Context chapter paints him as a representation of Renaissance man, encountering the limiting rules of religious belief. Consider the following views of Faustus's quest for power as stated by Stephen Orgel:

Marlowe starts with a fantasy of unlimited desire and unlimited power to satisfy it. When Faustus summons Mephistopheles, he articulates a megalomaniac dream – to live in all voluptuousness, to be the emperor of the world, to control nature and the supernatural. But [...] by the end of the same scene his voluptuousness has diminished significantly.

(S. Orgel in Kastan (ed.), *Doctor Faustus*, Norton Critical Editions, WW Norton & Co, 2005)

Mephistopheles effortlessly moves him on to what it turns out he really wants, books. The books are books of incantations, astronomy, and natural history: universal power is construed as power over the supernatural, the celestial, the natural, but epitomised in the written word – the power is literacy.

(S. Orgel in Kastan (ed.), *Doctor Faustus*, Norton Critical Editions, WW Norton & Co, 2005)

Activity 4

Having read Orgel's views on power in the play, to what extent do you agree that:

a) Faustus's incredible desires diminish in magnitude very quickly?

b) learning and literacy is the source of power?

Activity 5

Which of the following statements accurately sum up what the play shows about power? Where applicable, find supporting evidence from the play to justify these views.

> Power is shown to be an illusion. The powerful characters have much less power than at first appears.

> Human power is shown to be weak. As ever, time is the master of man.

> Even at the end, the play implies that God's power is above all others.

The power of religion

You have already explored the underlying religious concepts in the play in the Context chapter, so here you should consider how religion is represented in the text itself. Although the Pope and the powerful institution of the Catholic Church is mocked in Act III, for some readers there is also the sense that basic tenets of Christian salvation are endorsed.

Faustus mocks the Pope in a 2006 production

The Pope (who for the largely Protestant original audience was a figure of disdain) is the focus of comic ridicule. There is an element of **satire** at work in the Vatican scene, which highlights the purported folly of Catholic rituals. At this point in the text, the audience usually sides with Faustus, seeing the teasing as being well deserved. In the 2011 Shakespeare's Globe production, what shines through is the utter pomposity of religious power.

> **satire** humour used to make a serious point

As the procession enters in Act III Scene I, most performances make much of the pomp and ceremony of Catholicism. The bearing of crosiers and pillars are ironically held aloft as symbols of Christian belief, while at the same time a more earthly power struggle is being carried out. Faustus's trickery is straightforward visual comedy but no less funny for it. The stealing of food and wine perhaps is a perverse echo of the Eucharist, however the humour lies not in mockery of the particular rituals of Catholicism but in basic human matters such as theft of food and mild slapstick.

When Faustus hits the Pope, in some ways it seems a shockingly sacrilegious act but is often made funnier in performance by melodramatic reactions. The attempt of the Friars to exorcise the supposed demon with the excommunication ritual and chanting is shown to be ridiculous given the nature of what they chant, which sounds anything but religious. A deeper irony is at work, however: these Catholic rituals are ineffectual, whereas the satanic ones Faustus employs courtesy of Valdes and Cornelius seem more powerful.

Activity 6

How many of the Seven Deadly Sins are reflected in the characters of the play? Are all the sins of pride, covetousness, envy, wrath, gluttony, sloth and lechery represented in the attitudes and actions of the characters? Find examples for those that can be seen.

The representation of God offers some interesting interpretive challenges. The play is essentially about hell and its inhabitants. God is never seen on stage in the way Lucifer is, so God and the values ascribed to him are expressed through the words of others.

Activity 7

Consider the following lines from the play:

- **heavens conspired his overthrow** (Chorus, Prologue)

- **O, by aspiring pride and insolence,**
  For which God threw him from the face of heaven. (Mephistopheles, Act I Scene III)

- **Now, Faustus, must thou needs be damned,**
  And canst thou not be saved.
  What boots it then to think of God or heaven? (Faustus, Act II Scene I)

- **Ay, and Faustus will turn to God again.**
  To God? He loves thee not. (Faustus, Act II Scene I)

- **O, I'll leap up to my God! Who pulls me down?** (Faustus, Act V Scene II)

- **... see where God**
  Stretcheth out his arm and bends his ireful brows! (Faustus, Act V Scene II)

What impression of God is created in the above lines? Is God shown to be a forgiving, merciful entity or a vengeful, angry one? Is there any confirmation of these qualities in the text?

Activity 8

Consider how the original audiences might have perceived the representation of God. Carefully read the summary below. What is being said about the power balance between Faustus and God?

Elizabethan views of God and damnation

An Elizabethan view of religion complicates the position of Faustus because it suggests that Faustus did not have a choice about his actions – in other words, he was damned anyway before he made his pact.

Protestants wouldn't really accept the idea of devils acting of their own accord. Even though Mephistophilis ensnares Faustus, it was God's will, so ultimately it is God who damns Faustus.

Original audiences would have regarded it as God's decision as to whether Faustus is able to repent – it wouldn't be in Faustus's hands to decide.

Activity 9

Bearing in mind the points about Elizabethan views of God and damnation on p76 and your own views, how do you react to the following readings of God in the play? Which statements do you find most convincing?

> The absence of God in the play is significant. All we have are different characters' views projected onto an invisible entity. The ultimate conclusion must be that God doesn't exist: there is no salvation.

> The play shows the cruelty of God. Faustus's destiny is already determined and so all the advice of the Good Angel and the Old Man are hot air: Faustus is damned from the start.

> God emerges as the most powerful being in the world of the play. The infernal characters are his victims and right until the end his salvation is open to Faustus, who foolishly refuses it.

Some views of God's role suggest that human destiny is predetermined. While these beliefs are still held by some modern readers, the predominant view of life is that humans choose their direction: they can decide the path they take. Most of the early phase of the play shows Faustus justifying his choice to follow a diabolical path. The Old Man has clearly decided to follow the path of good.

Tips for assessment

Using criticism is a good way to strengthen your writing. Weaving in the views of others, including published critics, can lend depth to your analysis. Make sure that you use such material to illuminate and extend your arguments: never simply cite criticism – use it to bolster or challenge your own views.

React critically to criticism: never assume that a critic's view is necessarily 'right'. Think carefully about what it being said and consider whether you agree with a critical view.

The Old Man seems to be a physical version of the Good Angel, urging Faustus to make moral choices. It may strike you as telling that the forces of good seem distant characters: they are unnamed and symbolic rather than rounded characters. Marlowe makes the satanic characters much more immediate – the attractive rhetoric of Valdes and Cornelius, the energy of Mephistopheles and the frightening power of Lucifer seem much more interesting. In some ways, you might be able to understand why the path of goodness seems rather dull to Faustus.

Detail from a painting of heaven and hell by Hieronymus Bosch

The power of evil

In representing Lucifer on stage, the physical embodiment of evil, a director has some interesting choices to make. Do you present him as imperious and strikingly powerful, or do you show him as a hideous, damaged angel? The 2011 Shakespeare's Globe production presented him as an old, sickly, limping individual. In doing so, a director gives a reading of evil that suggests something unattractive. This raises an important question as to why Faustus isn't alerted to the obvious malign qualities of Lucifer, as signified by his physical impairment.

Mephistopheles first refers to 'Great Lucifer' in Act II and a few lines later Faustus uses the same **epithet**. Once again, you notice how the power of language is used to elevate and maintain the illusion. As becomes clear to the audience, Lucifer's power over God is questionable. Tellingly, when Faustus wavers in Act II Scene III, Lucifer appears and Faustus draws attention to his appearance: **'O, who art thou that look'st so terrible?'**. This appearance makes the wavering Faustus renew his pact. The promise of Lucifer to **'highly gratify'** Faustus is ironically followed by the cheap entertainment of the Seven Deadly Sins. Quite what Lucifer offers Faustus is questionable.

As you noticed in the Language chapter, hell is used literally and metaphorically at times. Faustus thinks hell is a fable but is curious to know more of it. When Mephistopheles proclaims **'Why, this is hell, nor am I out of it'** *(Act I Scene III)*, it could be read as an utterance of anguish or perhaps just a blunt acknowledgement of hell as a metaphor. Perhaps he means that hell is a state of mind – an inescapable recognition that salvation is beyond you.

---

epithet an adjective or phrase thought to describe someone aptly and used to criticise or praise them

The role of the individual

The play explores the position of the individual against that of wider spiritual and supernatural forces. The scope of the debate is whether man should know his place and stick to it, or whether he should rise above it. Is the spirit of Renaissance man being criticised in the play or does Marlowe present us with a man who in his failure still has a tragic grandeur?

The play invites you to take a position on what is being said about the right of the individual to push the boundaries. It might be that what the play says is at odds with your own thoughts as a human on the issue. One of the stumbling blocks in reading the play is the knowledge of Marlowe's supposed atheism. For some readers, it's hard to separate the apparent beliefs of the writer with the ideology of the text. Leo Kirschbaum makes the point passionately that 'there is no more obvious Christian document in all Elizabethan drama than Doctor Faustus':

> ... critics will consider the protagonist as a representative of the Renaissance superman. Whatever their feelings and thoughts on the revival of learning and the Reformation are, let them open-mindedly look at the play unfolding on the stage before them. For earthly learning, earthly power, earthly satisfaction, Faustus goes down to horrible and everlasting perdition. It does not matter what you think of Hell or what Marlowe privately thought of Hell. What does matter is that in terms of the play, Faustus is a wretched creature who for lower values gives up higher values.

(L. Kirschbaum, *Marlowe: Doctor Faustus*, Casebook Series, 1969)

Activity 10

How persuaded are you by Kirschbaum's argument? In the end, is the play simply a moral tale of a man who makes the wrong choices and pays for it?

If the role of the individual is held up for inspection and found wanting, what is at the root of his downfall? So far, you have considered Faustus's arrogance as the motivation for his actions. In the Context chapter, you looked at the parallels made with Icarus and Adam, and saw how the text offers a reading of man as overreacher. Some critics have argued that it is pride that brings about Faustus's fall – and it is his curiosity that drives his fatal actions. Faustus's intellectual and sensual behaviours are both linked to his curiosity. However, other characters in the play are fired up by curiosity, not just the protagonist.

Activity 11

a) How far is curiosity the determining feature of Faustus's conduct?

b) Which aspects of Faustus's sins might be deemed intellectual and which categorised as sensual?

c) Which other characters are driven by curiosity? Is it fair to say that all of the human characters are shown to be curious individuals?

Appearance and reality

Many stories concern themselves with the gap between what we perceive and how something actually appears. Some modern writers explore issues of identity and human self-perception, usually suggesting that how we see ourselves is different from how the world sees us. Renaissance dramatists made much of the theme, often exploiting dramatic irony for effect.

In *Macbeth*, for instance, the audience is made aware that Lady Macbeth plays the part of the welcoming hostess while secretly plotting murder.

In *Doctor Faustus*, the protagonist is very open about his desires and plans. Yet he himself often misreads situations or is seduced by outward appearance only to discover some horrific reality or benign,

Elizabeth Taylor as Helen in the 1967 film adaptation

dull truth. He assumes that his magical powers will bring him untold joy, yet the reality is that they seem to be mere distractions. The dreams of wealth and untold power diminish to the acquisition of books, some playful trickery and little else.

To Faustus, hell is a fable, as he famously proclaims. He discovers of course that it is a real place, both a mental and physical seat of torture. Helen is perhaps the most significant symbol of illusion. She appears beautiful, but brings death.

Activity 12

Make a list of the major characters in the text. Is there a gap between how they appear and the reality of their situation and conduct? You could use a table to record your notes as follows:

Character	Links to the theme of appearance and reality
Mephistopheles	His first appearance is too ugly for Faustus to endure and for the remainder of the play Faustus orders him to dress as a Franciscan friar. This is a conscious attempt on the part of the protagonist to hide the truth of his servant's identity. For his part, Mephistopheles appears to play the role of willing servant but is in truth trying to ensnare Faustus. His asides and dialogue with Lucifer reveal the truth of his intentions.

Activity 13

How do you react to the following view about appearance and reality in the play? Does it all seem accurate to you? Identify the parts you agree with and those you do not.

Faustus seems to be the most deluded character in the text. He is unable or unwilling to see Mephistopheles for what he is and this proves fatal. He allows himself to be drawn in by the lure of magic, another superficially attractive entity, which proves to be of lesser use. He is fooled by the supposed power of Lucifer, all the time being unaware of the power of God's salvation. Language is a trap for Faustus: he is seduced by his own fantasies and those of the magicians. The language of magic ensnares him, telling him he has power when all he does is hand power to Lucifer. The central message of the text seems to be a warning to be wary of one's own ability to see the truth of situations and that, in the end, the individual is fallible and foolish.

Writing about themes

Writing about themes and ideas is effective when you make links across the text and explore how themes are developed and added to as the play progresses. Being aware of how an idea is introduced, and then how it is repeated and expanded in later parts of the narrative is a useful way to bring together ideas about meanings and points about the playwright's method. Be alert to how one theme might be introduced mainly through one character's actions, but is then mirrored through another character. For instance, the idea of man misusing magic is first introduced through Faustus's actions, but is repeated and parodied through the actions of Wagner and then Robin.

Other structural ideas such as contrast are useful starting points for illuminating work on themes. For instance, you might compare the ways in which Faustus's obsession with Helen is also played out in Emperor Charles's fascination with Alexander.

The decisions made by a director and actors strongly influence the way a character or scene is received by the audience. If you read a novel, the action takes place in your head, but a drama script takes place on stage with the director and actors creating an interpretation of the play, one that may or may not coincide with the version you have in your head.

Marlowe's stage directions are minimal and so there is plenty of scope for how scenes may be performed and how lines may be delivered. As you study the play, be alert to the ways in which performance context can affect the way the play is interpreted. As ever, there is no 'correct' reading of the play.

Activity 1

Using theatrehistory.com as a starting point, explore the production history of the play. Are there any patterns in the way the play was produced in earlier centuries? *Doctor Faustus* has always been popular as a theatrical event. Which qualities lend themselves to performance?

Script and staging decisions

A key point to note about performances of the play is that what you might read on the page might not fully make it to the stage. The existence of two versions of the play and the subtle differences in various publications of the B text means that production teams have to decide which parts of the play they choose to work with.

In a play involving so many unrealistic entities, a challenge exists for a director: just how do you bring devils, magic and hell to the stage? Perhaps more importantly, how 'dark' should the play be? What should the relative balance be between the tragic and comic elements? In the 2016 RSC (Royal Shakespeare Company) version of the play, Maria Aberg made some key decisions about the direction of the play. Read the extracts below and on page 83 from her interview in *The Guardian*.

Directors of *Doctor Faustus* have two versions of the play to choose from – an 'A text' from 1604 and a 'B text' from 1616. Which have you used?

I lifted bits from both and cut it all quite substantially. I cut comedy scenes and wanted to focus on making it as dark as possible, streamlining the journey of Faustus. Both texts are dubious in origin. They're both slightly unreliable sources, which gives a director a bit of freedom to relate to them in a different way from a Tennessee Williams or whatever, where you know that everything on the page is a very accurate representation of the author's intentions.

> Productions of *Doctor Faustus* often struggle to balance the play's dark thrills with what you could charitably call its 'challenging' comic sequences.
>
> At the best of times, Elizabethan comedy is extremely difficult to pull off. I think if you're offsetting it against something quite complex, dark and brutal, it's even harder. For the story I wanted to tell, those scenes just really didn't interest me – partly because they don't feature Faustus and I wanted to make sure that he's in every scene.

(C. Wiegand, 'Your own personal demon: Maria Aberg on her *Doctor Faustus* double act', *The Guardian*, 12 February 2016)

Activity 2

How do you react to the director's justifications for cutting some of the comic scenes in the play? Do you imagine the theatrical experience and central meanings of the play would be strengthened by these decisions?

Activity 3

If you were charged with pruning the script of the play for performance, which scenes do you think might benefit from cutting and why?

Performance history: different productions

Being able to cite details of various performances over the centuries is of little use in itself, but noticing the general patterns or fashions for ways of staging the play and the concepts behind them can be illuminating. In general, performances of the play fall into one of two camps: those that presented the play as a story of a sympathetic Renaissance man crushed by the limits of his world and those that presented the play as a morality tale about a man who oversteps the mark.

Oliver Ryan as Mephistopheles and Sandy Grierson as Faustus in the RSC production, 2016

You might think that the play's focus on religious context ties the play to a historical timeframe, yet while the text references these issues, there are clearly elements of the play that have a universal appeal that transcends the socio-historical detail. At heart, the play is about power and humanity's place in the world. How the lead role is delivered is central to the way the play is received.

Read the following accounts of various productions:

I'm not sure that Benthall's version of the play was hard-hitting enough. Rather than a story of damnation, it was more like a tale of generally good chap who had made a small blunder and found himself in a pickle. Danemann's portrayal of Faustus was too honest and kind-hearted to convince me that he was a hellish rebel.

Eric Porter played Faustus superbly. Using his body language and facial expressions, it was clear to see the range of Faustus's character: he was simultaneously arrogant and bored, intelligent and cruel. He was a sort of Moriarty figure.

It was refreshing to see watch Christopher Fettes play the doctor as a young man, an adolescent even. The frustrations of Faustus came over as the frustrations of a late teenager. As music played, the audience watched Faustus the bored student smoking and interacting with his blind, wheelchair-bound tutor.

The supporting cast in Barry Kyle's 1989 production was composed of ten agile, young male actors. Dressed to emphasise their sexual energy, these actors played devils in the opening act and also doubled as scholars amongst others. They were devilish, shirtless and provocative.

Jude Law's Faustus seemed to be a rather spoilt young man – a brat. He wasn't sympathetic, instead his arrogance was brought to the fore. He was bitter and disparaging of other academics. By the end of the play, his scholarly clothing had been replaced by jeans and flowing white shirt, suggestive of a certain playboy lifestyle.

Activity 4

Of the five different performance versions of the play described above, which do you think offers the most appealing interpretation of the text? Is the play more interesting if Faustus is unsympathetic? Is Faustus a brat or a nice chap?

Performance as a reading

Period setting, costume, gesture, body language and delivery all contribute to performance and, in deciding such things, a reading of a text is produced. One way to explore the importance of performance context is to consider what sort of decisions you might make. Act I Scene III is a climactic part of the play where Faustus conjures Mephistopheles. In performance, many decisions have to be made that contribute to the overall effect. For instance:

- Faustus's first speech suggests symbols have been drawn on the floor. Should the effect be one of sinister darkness? How could lighting choices reflect this?

- How should the actor playing Faustus recite the Latin incantation? Should it be intoned deeply or should the audience be invited to see the actions as outmoded and a bit silly? What would happen if this were played with a knowing irony? Should Faustus's spell be immediately successful and how could the entry of Mephistopheles be performed? Is it possible or desirable that his appearance should seem frightening?

- In the dialogue between Faustus and Mephistopheles, how can the subtle power dynamics between the pair be brought out? Should Faustus's manner be imperious and egotistical to accompany his imperatives? When Mephistopheles disabuses Faustus of some of his notions, should the actor playing Mephistopheles adopt a dismissive tone? What should the body language between the two suggest?

- In Mephistopheles's explanation of hell, what range of emotions should the actor convey? Is anger the dominant tone when he says 'this is hell' (Act I Scene III)? Is the invocation to Faustus to cease performed in a heartfelt way? Should the audience think that Mephistopheles means what he says or should they be able to detect a hint of game-playing in his words?

Arthur Darvill portrays Mephistopheles in the 2011 Globe production

- When Faustus dismisses Mephistopheles's words of caution, should the audience perceive the Doctor as a fool? Should his speech here be accompanied by grandiose gestures? The speech has many powerful verbs and imperatives. Where would you advise the actor playing Faustus to pause or create emphasis in this speech – or should this be delivered in rapid fashion to suggest energy and verve?

- By the time Mephistopheles exits the stage, what should the power balance be between these characters? What does Mephistopheles's body language suggest? He is on stage for a lot of time, but speaks less than Faustus. What should the actor do in these silent moments? Is his body language still and powerful? Is his final line delivered with irony?

- Faustus's hyperbolic speech beginning '**Had I as many souls**...' praises Mephistopheles *(Act I Scene III)*. What sort of effect might this have on the audience? Are they meant to see him as a deluded fool at this point in the play? Or should his naïve excitement be sympathised with or even celebrated?

Activity 5

Think about Act I Scene III in light of the bullet points on pages 85-86. Then consider the following descriptions of two possible performances of Act I Scene III. Which, if either, chimes with how you view the scene?

- **Performance A:** The point of this scene is to suggest the folly of Faustus in conjuring Mephistopheles. The actions of Faustus appear slightly pompous at times, with a subtle tension between the elevated language of the Latin words of the spell and Faustus's slightly comic rejection of Mephistopheles's ugliness. It is clear that Mephistopheles plays the part of the servant, but his voice and body language suggest that he holds Faustus in low regard. The audience see this, but Faustus does not. Mephistopheles laughs as he exits.

- **Performance B:** It is crucial that the sinister horror of this scene is conveyed. The entrance of Mephistopheles is accompanied by a flickering of lights. Candles have been placed around the stage and a slightly nervous Faustus conducts the spell. A silence descends before dramatic lighting, sound and visual effects are used to present the entrance of Mephistopheles, who then delivers his words in a robotic way. A tension exists between the sinister stillness of Mephistopheles and Faustus's nervous energy.

Activity 6

Reread Act V Scene II and think about the different ways it might be performed. Write out two differing versions, using the model Performance A and Performance B above as templates.

Concepts underpinning performance

Most directors begin with an overall concept of the play and use this to inform key decisions about staging, costume and movement. Some productions are set in what might be considered a traditional way, adopting versions of 16th-century costume and using staging that suggests the religious and academic values of the time. Other directors select modern dress and place the text in a more contemporary world, which can help an audience to see the play through fresh eyes or perhaps make the point that the play's ideas are universal to any time.

Read the following accounts of two different productions of the play, both staged by the RSC. As you read, notice how staging and performance ideas help to convey psychological interpretations of the text.

Aberg's 2016 RSC production

At the start of this chapter you considered the editing decisions made by directors of the play. One of the defining features of Aberg's 2016 version concerned the striking of a match to determine which of the two central actors played Faustus and which Mephistopheles. Read Stephanie Mercier's account of this production:

 The two actors playing the lead parts entered black-suited on either side of the stage to face each other. Both struck a match and he who had the one that first extinguished played the part of Faustus. Here it was the cerebral Scottish Sandy Grierson; the more tensely physical Welsh Oliver Ryan played Mephistopheles. The random interchange device immediately raised levels of tension and electricity, provided an extra sense of danger and, as Ryan himself has pointed out, was an extremely efficient method of focusing, both for the actors and the audience.

(S. Mercier, *Doctor Faustus*, directed by Maria Aberg, The Swan Theatre, Stratford, 28 July 2016, front ground', 2016)

Sandy Grierson as Faustus and Oliver Ryan as Mephistopheles in the RSC production, 2016

This performance choice makes for an unusual and exciting start to the play, yet there is a wider concept underpinning this decision – one that suggests Faustus and Mephistopheles are mirror versions of each other. The concept of duality has been explored in several literary works (such as Stevenson's *The Strange Case of Dr Jekyll and Mr Hyde*), which suggest that human actions and behaviour include both good and evil, and that people are multifaceted in nature.

Aberg's production also hints at the issues of bipolarity and madness as central to Faustus's conduct. In his review of the performance, Andrew Duxfield noted other aspects of the production that support this concept:

- Both actors were dressed alike at the start of the play and had similar physical appearances.
- The colours used in most of the costumes were monochrome; for instance, Faustus dressed in black trousers and Mephistopheles in white trousers.
- The students of Faustus also doubled as the Devils in later scenes.
- The front cover of the programme featured Sandy Grierson looking into a mirror with Oliver Ryan's face looking back at him.
- The programme included a composite picture of the actor's faces, which merged into a single face.
- The programme also included a line from William Styron's *Darkness Visible: A Memoir of Madness*.

Activity 7

Consider the effect of Aberg's performance decisions. How might they link to and illuminate the following ideas arising from *Doctor Faustus*?

a) The various types of exchange in the play. How does the actors' exchange of roles reflect the other exchanges that take place in the narrative?

b) Faustus and Mephistopheles are closely linked in terms of desires and eventual outcomes.

c) Mephistopheles is an extension of Faustus's psyche rather than a separate character.

Another significant decision made by Aberg was the portrayal of Helen. In Act V Scene I, the initial depiction of this character was through a hazy video projection, which prevented the audience from fully visualising Helen's appearance. When she appeared on stage later in the scene, the effect was startling, as Andrew Duxfield notes:

There was, then, a palpable sense of audience discomfort when she emerged in the shape of a young girl […] As Helen approached, the tension was broken when the 'kiss' was replaced by a leaping embrace, like that of a daughter clinging to a father returned after a long absence […] Any relief was shortlived, however, as Faustus's disconnection from such innocence was given expression by Coot's Helen guiding his hands to her throat to force him to strangle her, and Faustus, after managing to release her unharmed, convulsing in the middle of the pentagram that he had earlier daubed on the stage; the overall effect was to transform the scene from one about desire and lust to one about grief and loss.

(A. Duxfield, 'Review of Marlowe's *Doctor Faustus* (directed by Maria Aberg for the Royal Shakespeare Company) at The Swan Theatre, Stratford-upon-Avon, 9 June 2016')

 Activity 8

Given the decisions made by Aberg about the depiction of Helen, consider the following questions.

a) Why might the audience have felt discomfort about her youthfulness?

b) What could the action of Helen forcing Faustus to strangle her signify?

c) Does the feeling of grief and loss created in this production of the scene reflect your own reading of the play?

Barton's 1974 RSC production

John Barton's 1974 RSC version of the play, with Ian McKellen as Faustus, was first performed at the Edinburgh Festival and then toured some UK theatres. The concept for this performance was that the action was all in the head of a psychotic Faustus.

Puppets were used to represent the Sins, the Angels and other characters with the central idea being that the drama occurred inside the mind of Faustus. Barton chose to set the play in Faustus's study – the Chorus was used to tell the audience of Faustus's supposed adventures around the globe.

The set had the appearance of the inside of a skull with dark alcoves and sloping walls, emphasising the idea that the action was in the doctor's mind. The opening Chorus was given to Lucifer to speak and on Faustus's desk sat an hourglass counting down to his doom.

The physical appearance of Faustus changed during the play. His manner of a well-dressed, youthful and beardless academic in the first half gave way to a bearded, careworn and grey old man. None of the comedy scenes were used.

Interestingly, the roles of Valdes and Cornelius were played by Beelezebub and Mephostophilis, suggesting their connection to the diabolical world. The Chorus was composed of devils and the Angels were mere puppets, operated by Faustus himself.

The moment of death was understated: some productions ramp up the spectacle. In this version, Faustus simply fell to the floor, twitching. His scholar's robes remained in his chair. No devils appeared, nobody dragged him to hell. Faustus lay on the floor, as lifeless as the puppets he operated.

Activity 9

How do you view Barton's version of the play as the fantasy of a mentally ill man? What is added by:

a) the choice to only use one setting? How does it fit in with the overall concept?

b) the set design and the decision to have Lucifer speak the Prologue?

c) the cutting of the comic scenes and the change in costume?

d) the use of puppets operated by Faustus?

e) the downplayed ending?

Tips for assessment

You will never be asked to simply describe a performance of *Doctor Faustus* that you have seen or read about. However, by briefly referring to how particular staging effects enhance the meaning of a certain line, or section of text, you can use your performance knowledge to demonstrate a deeper understanding of the text. For example, when Ian McKellen uses puppets for the Angels, this raises questions about whether Marlowe intended the Angels to be real or simply figments of Faustus's imagination.

Activity 10

Explore ways in which you might stage Act V Scene II to bring out the full drama of Faustus's last hour. In particular, think about how much energy the actor should bring to the scene. What should be the balance between despair and resistance?

McKellen's Faustus confronted by the Good Angel, in puppet form, in the RSC production, 1974

Activity 11

Mephistopheles can be played in a variety of ways. Select some keys scenes involving this character and experiment with how action, delivery of lines and body language might bring out different interpretations of his character. Start by deciding whether he is a potentially tragic character who deserves pity or a sinister, malevolent force who destroys Faustus.

Performing spectacle

One of the challenges for a director is to decide how to handle the numerous spectacles in the play. *Doctor Faustus* requires the deployment of theatrical devices such as fireworks and apparitions, not least in the performance of the Seven Deadly Sins. In the play, their appearance aims to distract Faustus from the difficult questions he asks. The implication is that their visual appearance needs to be dramatically striking. In the 2011 Shakespeare's Globe production, the Sins emerged from a trapdoor, with Lechery appearing as a temptress, perhaps making a structural link with Helen. Read Maria Aberg's explanation of how she staged this scene in the 2016 RSC production:

In the A text, the seven deadly sins appear without any real dramaturgical necessity, as a bit of entertainment. I restructured the text because I wanted to make sure that they were used to convince Faustus that he is making the right decision, so they had to represent something that he really wanted but wouldn't have experienced in his life as an academic: they had to be seductive, exciting, thrilling – overwhelming in some sense for him as a character. [...] It felt like it needed to be something fun, dangerous and seductive without being slick.

(C. Wiegand, 'Your own personal demon: Maria Aberg on her *Doctor Faustus* double act', *The Guardian*, 12 February 2016)

Activity 12

Look again at Act II Scene III where the Seven Deadly Sins appear. What decisions would you make about costume and movement? How would you bring out the various personalities of these characters?

Another key decision in terms of spectacle is how to perform the final moment of Faustus's life. For example, in Clifford Williams's 1968 RSC production, some reviewers felt there was a cruelty in the way that the play ended. Once his final speech was delivered, Faustus fell to the ground, whimpering in mortal fear. But then nothing happened – the clock finished striking and a moment lingered. Faustus laughed, almost as if he had got away with it. Then with a swift cruelty, the rear wall of stage collapsed to reveal the fiery glow of Hell. Figures from the underworld slowly surrounded the doctor and carried him to Hell, at which point, the rear wall of the set returned to position.

Activity 13

In Williams's version of the ending, what is achieved by having a pause between the final clock strike and the appearance of the denizens of hell? Does Williams's version capture the horror of the moment in your opinion?

Filmed versions of the play

Film versions offer a different opportunity to play with the text, often altering dialogue or having the luxury to switch quickly between the sorts of lavish sets that can't be reproduced on stage. The 1967 film version of the play featuring Richard Burton and Elizabeth Taylor (as Helen) was not well received, yet it does offer some interesting nuances, most notably presenting Faustus's motivation in a different way to the printed version.

One of the distinguishing features is the concept that Faustus isn't driven by intellectual desires, but sensual ones. The eye of the skull sitting on his desk offers him visions of naked females. The set itself resembles a trashy horror film, complete with dangling spider webs, garish lighting and disembodied voices.

The poster for the theatrical release on the 1967 film adaptation, directed by Richard Burton and Nevill Coghill

Writing about performance

Upgrade

In your writing, you will need to use performance context carefully. There is no advantage in listing features of various productions you may have seen unless it is directly relevant to the question that faces you. Writing about performance works best when linked to the overarching concepts and ideas in the play. If you are exploring an extract from *Doctor Faustus* closely, you may well choose to focus on a specific key line from the text and write about various ways the performance of the line might give rise to different readings of character. Be careful not to confuse the study of literature with theatre studies – the primary focus is the text and its meanings. Dramatic method and performance aspects should only support the points you make about the literary aspects of the play.

Doctor Faustus has generated many critical responses. The changing contexts in which the play is performed and received have ensured that the play has a long critical history. Literary criticism can illuminate your understanding of the play and help you view its content from different angles, but it is also perfectly acceptable to disagree with views. Careful reading and assessment of criticism is very important. This chapter offers ways into handling critical study.

Activity 1

As a starting point for your study of critical views, research early responses to *Doctor Faustus*, such as those from William Hazlitt (in *Lectures on the Age of Elizabeth*, 1820) and A.C. Bradley (in *The English Poets: Selections with Critical Introductions*, 1880).

Reading positions and approaches

Critical opinions about texts are personal responses, but they are never free from the cultural baggage and prejudices of the person who writes them. Although it is tempting to read critical opinion as simply a person's individual response, each response embodies the values of the person and society in which it is written. The approach critics adopt says a lot about what they think is the 'correct' or most illuminating way to read literature.

Essentialist criticism, an older approach that analysed characters as though they were 'real', has largely been overtaken by approaches that see literature as **representational**. This means judging characters and texts as representations of society. Therefore, the task of the reader is to look at the representation offered in the text and to explore the ideology (view of the world) it proposes.

essentialist looking for the essence of a character itself, as though the character had a 'real' existence

representational seeing characters and situations as constructs – versions of 'real' characters and events. Representational readings place emphasis on how they have been shown by the author and what they reveal about the values of society and the author

Opposite are two central approaches or schools of thought on how literature can be read.

Marxist criticism

Marxist criticism takes its cue from political beliefs originating in the views of Karl Marx, an economist and philosopher. Adopting a Marxist approach to reading literature means:

- exploring the representation of power, class and status in the world of the text. Marx's view was that economic situations determine everything in the real world. This means that analysing the interaction of social and economic factors in the text, and also the conditions in which the text was produced, is central to any reading

- acknowledging that human beings are less free than they might think and that what we might think as 'the way the world works' is an illusion. The prevailing ideology is designed by those in power to keep them in power. The powerless, by contrast, see this ideology as 'common sense' and 'normal' rather than anything that could be challenged. Consequently, Marxist critics look closely at issues of conflict, ideology and class struggle in the world of the text.

Gender criticism

Gender criticism looks at the ways literature represents masculinity and femininity. Readers exploring texts from this angle take the view that:

- literature can promote negative images of gender, helping to support stereotypes rather than challenge them. Females, for example, might be portrayed in narrow roles: as virginal or whorish, helpless or shrewish. Exploring the depiction of both genders can reveal a lot about the way society and the writer view men and women

- many texts considered 'literary' are written by men for men. There is an assumption that the general reader is male and that the sorts of texts promoted by educational institutions are mainly the work of dead white males. Feminist critics explore and expose the view that to be male and heterosexual is 'normal' and to be female or gay is to be 'different'.

Activity 2

Consider the role of power and status in the play. You could examine:

- the power structures in Faustus's house. How does the dialogue between Faustus and Wagner reflect the way power operates? Does the power shift when Mephistopheles enters the play?

- the relative power of the infernal characters. What do you notice about the relationship between Lucifer and Mephistopheles? Do you see this as a play that explores hierarchies and suggests that they can't ultimately be overturned?

Activity 3

Consider the role of gender in the play. You could consider:

- what masculinity means in the play. How much of it is bound up with toughness and power? Are men ever 'weak' in the text? If so, what happens to them? Is Faustus a coward in his final scene?

- how the minimal role of females in the play could be presented. Should Lechery be represented as a sluttish female? What gender(s) should the Good and Evil Angel be? What effect might be created by having an all-male cast? Here you might contrast modern production choices with the effect created by Elizabethan stage versions of the play, which would have used boys and men to play the female roles.

 Activity 4

There are many other critical theories and approaches that can inform your study of *Doctor Faustus*. Some theoretical approaches are relatively new and still evolving. Some approaches are complex and demand careful study. Research the following areas and their potential usefulness to your reading of the play:

- Post-colonialism
- Eco-criticism
- Narrative and narratology
- Postmodernism
- Psychoanalytical.

Beginning to apply critical views

As you begin to explore published critical views, take time to understand the arguments being proposed, the approach being taken and, crucially, whether you agree with what is being said. Use the next activities to hone your skills.

 Activity 5

Read Text A opposite carefully. Consider:

- Is Faustus an egotist who dismisses his critics?
- Is there textual evidence to say Faustus wallows in his sense of worth?

Use Text B to practise your critical reading skills. Read the interpretation and then:

- list the key points being made about Faustus's character
- find references and events in the play to support or challenge the reading proposed
- write a response, pulling your points and evidence together, which considers how convincing you think the opinion of Faustus is.

TEXT A

Faustus is wholly egocentric. To himself, he is either the greatest of men, or the greatest of abject sinners. He underrates his opponents, and relishes his inflated sense of his own abilities. Thus, after Mephistopheles has left the stage at the behest of the magician in the more pleasant guise of a Franciscan [...] Faustus wallows in a delusion of self-importance.

(L. Kirschbaum, 'Religious Values in *Doctor Faustus*', *Twentieth-Century Interpretations of Doctor Faustus,* 1969)

TEXT B

From the very beginning Marlowe's Faustus is too much a stiff-necked pursuer of his own way to be all that he should be as a figure of man in a medieval Morality play. We do not see a typical Morality play temptation by a figure of evil, whether man or devil prevailing upon an innocent Faustus [...] we see a knowing Faustus deliberately setting himself upon an evil course.

(W. Farnham, *Twentieth-Century Interpretations of Doctor Faustus,* 1969)

Interpreting Faustus: further views

You have seen how it is possible to respond to Faustus in a variety of ways. In Text C, Susan Snyder proposes an interesting opinion about the nature of Faustus's journey. In Text D, R. B. Sewell considers how Faustus represents anyone with talent and imagination.

Activity 7

Read Texts C and D on the next page. Consider these questions:

a) If Faustus's journey in the narrative can be read as the inversion of a saint's life, then which parts of the story correspond to the elements Snyder identifies?

b) How far do you agree that justice isn't served at the end of the text?

TEXT C

The saint's life is a didactic biography [...] containing some or all of the following elements: early life (sometimes worldly and sinful), conversion to God, sacramental reception into the church, struggle against various temptations of the devil (sometimes overcome with the direct aid of God or his agents), miracles and mystic experiences (sometimes climaxed by a form of the beatific vision), holy death. Doctor Faustus turns the whole pattern upside down.

(S. Snyder, 'Marlowe's *Doctor Faustus* as an inverted saint's life', *Doctor Faustus*, Norton Critical Editions, 2005)

TEXT D

If he is more sinning than sinned against, he yet has shown great capacities of good as well as evil, and we cannot feel that perfect justice has been done. Theologically, of course, Faustus in his extremity was mistaken: it is never too late to receive God's mercy and pardon [...] But the final scene gives a sense, not so much of the justice and goodness of the universe as of the transcendent individual, caught in the consequences of a dilemma which, granted the conditions of his times, it was impossible for any imaginative man wholly to avoid.

(R. B. Sewell, *The Vision of Tragedy*, Paragon House, 1990)

Interpreting farce

In these next pieces of criticism, the writers explore the value of the comedy and how it can be viewed in the body of the play. Thinking about the play as a blend of genres is something you have been doing throughout this book, so now consider the effectiveness of the comedic elements.

Activity 8

Read Texts E and F opposite carefully and consider:

a) whether the effect of both plots descending into trivialities is an effective development

b) why some critics might have reacted negatively to these trivialities

c) whether the comedy helps you come to a moral judgment about Faustus

d) if the comedy is well executed enough to make you laugh.

TEXT E

It is not only in the detail of individual scenes that the subplot parodies the main plot: the whole movement of the subplot mirrors that social and intellectual descent that I have traced in the career of Faustus. The first subplot scene concerns Wagner, a man close to Faustus himself. The second comic scene involves Wagner and his servants [...] The third and subsequent scenes show [them] by themselves, Wagner now having disappeared [...] At both levels the action descends to trivialities and the critics close their eyes in dissent.

(G. K. Hunter, 'Five-Act Structure in *Doctor Faustus*', *Doctor Faustus*, Norton Critical Editions, 2005)

TEXT F

It is only after the farcical stage action has finished that we step back and make moral judgments on Faustus's share in the action. Before that, we are too closely involved in following the twists and turns of the plot, or in laughing at its outcome. Whoever wrote the fourth act of Doctor Faustus was a consummate comedian, who understood not only the traditions of the genre which the play is working in, but also how to manipulate audience response.

(M. Mangan, *Doctor Faustus*, Penguin Critical Studies, 1989)

Tips for assessment

Don't worry that you need to learn long passages of critical thought. Jot down any really interesting ideas you come across to create a 'key critical ideas' list that you could refer to when you write practice responses. Integrating critical ideas into your revision work means you will be more confident about doing this in the exam.

Faustus signs his soul over to Lucifer

Interpreting narrative

Rather than focus upon character or theme, some criticism looks at the way in which texts are structured and the effects that are generated. Texts G and H look at how the playwright's choices of subtitle, plot and subplot, entrances and dialogue impact the play.

Activity 9

Read Texts G and H below. Consider whether:

a) you think Marlowe is parodying the morality play genre

b) it is possible to divide the characters up into different orders.

TEXT G

By 1590 the full apparatus of Morality was an old and musty form of drama [...]
I believe Marlowe's adoption of Morality form must be seen as a deliberate mis-use of popular old-fashioned material. There are two possible forms this mis-use might have taken: firstly, to present Faustus as a simple Morality story, and to give it a bitter ironic twist right through [...] the other possible mis-use of the Morality form is to invert it completely to portray the search of a man for Hell not Heaven.

(N. Brooke, 'The Moral Tragedy of *Doctor Faustus*',
Marlow: Doctor Faustus, Casebook Series, 1969)

TEXT H

There are in this one play four sets of orders of persons: (1) the purely abstract and symbolic, such as Lucifer, who only appear on an upper stage at certain moments, and take no part in the action; (2) the intermediate, for instance Mephistopheles, who ought to be symbolic but treads the lower stage, a cowled enigma, horrible because at moments he ceases to be symbolic without becoming human; (3) the heroic or tragic: Faustus, who is an ideal half-realised, hanging together on its own plane; (4) the real: common mortals who would attract no attention.

(F. MacDonald Cornford, 'View Point',
Twentieth-Century Interpretations of Doctor Faustus, 1969)

Interpreting universal experience

Literature can be read as reinforcing moral messages that are universal to the people who read it. For instance, a straightforward reading of *Doctor Faustus* might suggest that necromancy is not to be pursued. The play may also be seen as a metaphor for the way that humans handle change, in particular how shifts in social and ideological systems can cause chaos for the individual.

Activity 10

Text I offers a view on the human experience. It suggests that Faustus rejects human values in the end. Read the text and consider whether:

a) Faustus's Helen speech is nostalgic for a bygone past

b) the play can be read as an individual failing to cope with changing times

c) Faustus consciously rejects humanity through his actions.

TEXT I

He finds himself employed as an entertainer to the Emperor whom he had earlier hoped to control, and finds himself pensioned off at the conclusion of the evening's show […] such sustained contrasts between the plot which Faustus gets and the plot which he has envisioned for his life constitute another of the effective ironies of the tragedy. The demands for knowledge and for power finally cease, and the last request is for Helen – the demon-lover – who becomes an existential symbol for the repudiation of creation and for Faustus's 'marriage' with Hell.

(R. M. Frye, 'Marlowe's *Doctor Faustus*: the repudiation of humanity', *Twentieth-Century Interpretations of Doctor Faustus*, 1969)

Oliver Ryan in Maria Aberg's stage version of the play at The Swan Theatre, 2016

Interpreting disunity

Throughout this book you have been weighing up *Doctor Faustus* and trying to reach some decisions about its message, its central character and its genre hybridity. It is natural to wish to decide firmly on a single meaning of the play. Yet in many ways, the play is an unstable text: there are numerous versions of it, disagreement about how to classify it, and the issue of whether it is irrevocably tied to the socio-historical issues at the time of its production.

Many contemporary approaches to literature draw attention to the fault lines in texts. Rather than try to find a unified message in a text, postmodern approaches to reading argue that because life is a random, unpatterned experience, then literature is too. Readers in this school of thought deny that texts have fixed stable meanings, despite human desire to impose a meaning on a text. This approach to reading may seem odd given the attempts of this book to offer interpretations, yet you may wish to explore further the gaps and fragmentary nature of *Doctor Faustus*.

 Activity 11

Read Text J, which argues that the instability at the heart of the play is actually central to the meaning of the play. Think carefully about the points it makes, specifically whether:

a) there is actually a structural unity to the play

b) instability is reflected in the construction of the play and its protagonist

c) you accept the unstable nature of the text and its meanings, or whether you seek a fixed interpretation.

 TEXT J

Instability is fundamental in the play, as a theme and a characteristic. Faustus is a play of violent contrasts within a rigorous structural unity. Hilarity and agony, seriousness and irresponsibility: even on the most cautious theories of authorship, Marlowe is responsible at times for all these extremes. This artistic instability matches the instability of the hero. The extremes of optimism and depression, enthusiasm and hatred, commitment to Hell and aspiration to Heaven, pride and shame: these are the swings of the pendulum in Faustus's world, and they are reflected by the sickening to-and-fro motion of the verse.

(J. B. Steane, 'Faustus: a great work flawed',
Twentieth-Century Interpretations of Doctor Faustus, 1969)

Developing your own readings

Critical views are useful in provoking thought and inviting you to look at the play from different angles. They should be exercised with caution and engaged with, rather than taken as 'correct' viewpoints'. The most important view of the play's elements is your own. Any response you give to the play will ultimately be your own view, although it may well be informed by those of other readers and published critical opinions.

Part of the process of generating your own opinion of the play may be helped by applying the different reading approaches mentioned at the start of this chapter. While there are different types of gender and Marxist criticism, considering how these sorts of approaches might make you see the play in different ways can be a useful starting point.

Activity 12

a) Reread Act V Scene I. Consider how different reading approaches might help you generate views of this part of the play. Use the following prompts.

- Explore the representations of gender in this extract. What significant aspects of masculinity and femininity are shown? Is it possible to say that familiar stereotypes of men and women are employed in the presentation of Helen and the Old Man?

- Look closely at the nature of power and status. What is shown about the way social structures operate? Look at the nature of Faustus's interactions with the Scholars and Mephistopheles as a starting point.

b) Using your observations, write a close analysis of Act V Scene I in terms of the issues relating to gender and power. Adopt a critical approach you think best suits the way you wish to interpret the play. Use Texts A–J (pages 97-102) as models of the way in which you might write your response.

Writing about critical views

When you read criticism in conjunction with *Doctor Faustus*, you are effectively juggling two texts. Critical views are essentially 'writing about writing' and are, in the end, just views. Rather than taking a critical view at face value, it is important that you first of all understand what is being said and, secondly, that you evaluate it. Read criticism *critically*. You should test views out and see if you agree with them – or not. Never just refer to a view. Look at the strengths and weaknesses of the reading.

Exam skills

Writing about any literary text involves a set of key skills that you will need to practise and master. Insightful, effective responses about any piece of literature are grounded in your understanding of the text. During the course of your studies, you must ensure that you are confident about the plot, structure, characters, settings, themes and genre elements of *Doctor Faustus*. This will enable you to select wisely the material you want to focus upon, ensuring you choose the most fruitful aspects of the text to explore in your writing.

Whether you set your own questions or respond to tasks given to you, writing about *Doctor Faustus* at A/AS level requires you to work on your phrasing skills, take account of dramatic method, context and genre, and, most importantly, focus closely on the question you are presented with. Invariably, A/AS-level tasks will ask more specific questions, sometimes offering debates to respond to or an extract to comment on. The quality of your ideas, the strength of your argument and your own personal voice will be central to any piece of writing you construct. Refining your thinking and discussion skills is essential.

Focusing on the task

Questions, or tasks as they are often termed, require an answer. The wording of a task is carefully crafted to stimulate your thoughts and point you in certain directions. Ignoring the task and simply writing 'everything I know about the play' will result in a poor essay. Similarly, taking a question and warping it so you can write about what you know best (rather than respond to the actual question you've been given) will also have a disastrous outcome. Focusing on the task in hand and looking at the key words is the starting point of an effective answer.

Activity 1

Look carefully at the following task. What are the key words? What precisely is the task inviting you to do?

> How far do you agree that Marlowe presents Faustus as an egotistical character for whom the audience feels no sympathy?

The first thing you might have noticed is the invitation to offer an opinion. This is carried in the words: 'How far do you agree…'. The use of the second person pronoun should alert you to the fact that this type of task isn't asking what somebody in Marlowe's time thought or what a variety of readers might think but, crucially, is asking for *your* opinion. It is therefore important that your response does provide *your* opinion, and you must come to a conclusion.

The first five words also tell you that there is some sort of debate being set up. There are two strands to the debate. The first opinion you are given to react to is the view that Faustus is 'egotistical' and then, allied to that, the view that the audience 'feels no sympathy for him'. It is possible to take issue with or support one or both of these readings of the play and so any effective essay will need to work very closely to build an argument around these key terms.

The term 'sympathy' introduces both a genre and a cultural concept – that of judgment of character. In tragic literature, 'egotistical' signifies someone whose flaws may well lead to disaster. To answer this question, you would also have to bring in your own cultural understanding of what grounds for 'sympathy' constitute. Here, there will be differences between readers in what 'deserving sympathy' might mean: literature, as ever, asks you to decide where your moral boundaries lie. You can see how some of the ways you might interpret the words and actions of the characters are open to interpretation, and this task is asking how you see that. Is Faustus 'egotistical'? Is it accurate to say the audience feels no sympathy? Or is there something more complex about the way you react to the protagonist?

Another aspect of the task is carried in the words 'Marlowe presents'. Here you are being reminded that there is a playwright who carefully shapes and arranges the material. You are being asked to look at how the playwright structures the text: what he has the characters doing in relation to unruly behaviour, the exits and entrances, the character arc, the words used, etc. Remember that writing about method doesn't mean *writing anything* about method: it must be relevant to the task, so any points you make about method must serve the key terms 'egotistical' and 'feels no sympathy'.

In summary, the task requires you to debate the ideas that Faustus is egotistical and unsympathetic, and think about the playwright's methods as you do so. Implicit in all of this are the assumptions that you will write clearly and fluently, and use evidence – quotations or references – to support your points.

Tips for assessment

Writing effective essays shouldn't be reduced to a checklist. Formulaic responses run the risk of being straitjacketed, rather than interesting and creative. It is possible, however, to use the following prompts to judge the quality of your own work.

- How closely do I focus on the key terms in the task?
- How well do I get involved in the debate?
- What is the quality of my argument? How convincing is it?
- Is my essay well structured and fluently written?

Activity 2

Using the prompt list on the previous page, read the following extracts from student responses and judge the quality of each answer. They are both partial answers to the following task.

> How far do you agree that Marlowe presents Faustus as an egotistical character for whom the audience feels no sympathy?

Extract 1

Doctor Faustus does seem to be an unlikeable character. It appears that he has devilish plans and will stop at nothing to get what he wants. In the Prologue he is described as being from 'base of stock', which suggests that he has had a spectacular rise to become a doctor. This might explain why he wishes to control the world and learn the evil art of necromancy. In the play, he doesn't listen to advice – he does what he wants. Some of his actions are funny, such as the scene where he boxes the Pope's ears. To some people watching the play at the time it was written, this would have been offensive but to some, it would have been hilarious. The story shows how he over-reached his limits and caused his own downfall, becoming a tragic figure.

Extract 2

If we choose to interpret the play as a tragic text, then some degree of sympathy for Faustus is essential: in order to bring out the protagonist's tragic suffering, then we need to see him as partially sympathetic. Marlowe cleverly manipulates our attitude to Faustus by inviting us to see why he appears egotistical: he is an intelligent man who is trapped by the values of the world he finds himself in. This alone is enough to engender sympathy. When Marlowe has Faustus declare 'Divinity, adieu!', the audience may well see his egotism, but they also warm to the libertarian Renaissance man who refuses to be bound. Consequently, as the futility of Faustus's offer to 'burn my books' is uttered, it is impossible not to feel sympathy: we are witnessing the crushing of the human spirit by uncaring forces.

As you read the student responses, you will have noticed both are written in clear English and show understanding of the play and its events. But you will hopefully have noticed that the second response is better. Reread the responses in conjunction with the following commentaries.

Commentaries on extracts from student answers

Extract 1 doesn't really focus on the key debate. The student has overlooked the central aspect in the question – egotism – and chosen to write about Faustus in a general way, rather than focusing sharply on the task. Once this error has occurred, it becomes difficult for the student to show their abilities, and difficult to reward the answer. There is an indirect attempt to look at Faustus's manner, however: the basic idea that he won't listen to advice. Once again, though, the student adopts a loose approach to the key terms and treats them in a general way; there is a feeling that they are writing some things about the character that have some relevance in places. There is some sense that this is a drama with an audience but no real grasp of Marlowe's method. A quotation is used to illustrate a basic point, but the whole response is undermined by the inability to see what the question requires.

Extract 2 has a much tighter grasp on the task. The focus on sympathy is present all the way through and the student chooses a sensible part of the play to explore this question. Some thoughtful points around 'egotistical' are offered, with the convincing example of Faustus's dialogue being well used to illustrate this. There is a sense that the dramatic qualities of the play are brought out and the wider tragic ideas such as suffering are being considered. The student has a strong personal view, which posits that for tragedy to work, sympathy is essential. Quotations aren't extensive but are judiciously chosen and the phrasing is fluent. The strength of this response is that it approaches the debate head on and organises the answer around the key terms in the task.

Activity 3

Write your own paragraph to the task you explored in actvity 1. Choose different examples to those used in Extract 2 to support your view.

Planning and structuring an answer

At A/AS level, planning and thinking before you write becomes even more important. A coherent, well-structured response does not happen unless some degree of forethought occurs. As you saw above, focusing closely upon the key terms and structuring an answer around them is essential. Once you've identified the point of the task, it makes sense to do the following:

1 Think carefully about the whole narrative of the play. Which parts of it – which events and scenes – are going to be most useful in helping you to answer the task? If you are engaging with a debate, are there parts of the play that show the character or theme in different lights?

2 Jot down a list of points you wish to make, ensuring that every one of them serves the question. Resist any temptation to show off knowledge that isn't relevant to the question.

3 Choose some quotations to employ in the body of the essay.

4 Work out a 'route through' your essay. It may well be that in a debate-style task, you begin by looking at the main view proposed in the task, and then move on to consider alternative views.

5 Work out what your conclusion would be. Your conclusion needs to be a strong statement that gives your definitive answer to the task. The best writing is often committed to a certain view, but acknowledges the contrasting or conflicting elements of the debate.

6 Use your conclusion to help you write your introduction.

Writing convincing introductions

A good introduction should signpost an argument. Ideally, the person who reads your work should be able to get a sense of what your argument is going to be. If you plan your answer properly and know what your conclusion will be, then you can signal it in your introduction.

Activity 4

Compare these two introductions to the following question. Which is the more effective, and why?

How far do you agree that the comic scenes in the play are a distraction from the tragic scenes?

Sample introduction 1

Doctor Faustus was probably written by more than one person. Some of the scenes focus on darker ideas and some of them focus on comic ones. The comic ones are mainly in Acts 3 and 4, although the earlier scenes with Robin are funny too. Comedy is used to make people laugh and this is the case in *Doctor Faustus*, although the ending isn't funny. Perhaps Marlowe decided that the ending needed to show that the central character had to be punished for his sins.

Sample introduction 2

The hybridity of *Doctor Faustus* can seem unusual to many readers, yet it is quite easy to see how, rather than being a distraction, the comic scenes actually support and enhance the meanings of the play. The comedy offers much more than simple relief: it serves to show the debasement of Faustus and also echoes some events in the tragic plot. In blending elements of two genres, tragedy and comedy, Marlowe offers a text that is strikingly modern, whose variety is very much a strength.

Choosing quotations

One of the arts you need to master is that of selection. In a play containing many memorable lines, being able to select the most telling quotation to help you clinch a point is essential. Quotations may only be a few words in length, but should be judiciously chosen. Lengthy quotations often get in the way of a good point. Embed short quotations within the body of your paragraphs, using them as ways to sum up a point or as a springboard to move on.

Activity 5

If you were required to answer the task in Activity 4, which lines or phrases would you select from *Doctor Faustus* to support or challenge the view given? What would your argument be?

Activity 6

Using the skills you have practised so far, plan an answer to the following task:

> To what extent do you agree that Marlowe presents Mephistopheles as nothing more than a deeply sinister and malevolent character?

You should:

a) select the most relevant parts of the text to write about

b) work out what your argument would be

c) select useful quotations

d) make a list of the points you would make, in order

e) write a coherent introduction and conclusion.

Activity 7

Now write an answer to the task you planned in Activity 6.

Sample answers

Activity 8

a) Read Sample answers 1 and 2, which are extracts from two student responses to the question you planned in Activity 6. Then read the annotations and concluding commentary on each response.

b) Compare the essay you wrote in Activity 7 to the sample answers. Is it more like Sample answer 1 or 2? How might you set about improving your response?

Sample answer 1

> To what extent do you agree that Marlowe presents Mephistopheles as nothing more than a deeply sinister and malevolent character?

Mephistopheles is in league with the devil, which obviously makes him a sinister figure. In the play, Mephistopheles appears when Faustus conjures him. He enters, then re-enters as a Franciscan friar after Faustus says he is too ugly. His first act is to try to persuade Faustus to think again, but then he makes sure that he gives his soul to Lucifer. This is clearly a sinister act.

Malevolent basically means evil, and this is true because tempting someone to lose their life is a sinister act. In many ways, he is a friend though. Faustus doesn't appear to have many people to confide in, so it could be said that he's not just sinister. They have many conversations – Faustus learns from him.

They also have fun together, for instance when they visit Europe and play tricks on people, like the Pope. There are scenes where they dress up, steal food and frighten people. They also work together like a team, for example, in the scene where they produce 'ripe grapes' for the Duchess of Vanholt. They seem to be good friends and although Mephistopheles is trying to drive Faustus to hell, they also seem to be quite close.

The opening sentence gives a view, but it's a little blunt.

Most of this paragraph spends too much time retelling the story. There is no real sense that an argument is being constructed yet.

There is the beginning of a counterview here, which would have benefited from further thought and detail.

The details chosen to make this point are imprecise.

The story is being retold again in this part of the essay. The quotation doesn't really add much to the argument.

Throughout this paragraph, the student writes about the characters as if they are real rather than constructs of the playwright.

This is a thoughtful point, but it needed more exploration.

Another way of looking at the character is that he has some inner sadness. In the first part of the play, Mephistopheles confesses that he is disappointed to have been thrown from heaven, so he might not just be a malevolent character. Another idea might be that the writer wants us to see how Faustus is unable to understand that he is being tricked, so there's a bit of a gap between how Faustus sees his servant and how the audience does.

The essay ends with another potentially interesting idea that could have been developed.

This response operates at a simple level. There is some focus on the debate, but no real depth to the argument. For the most part, the characters are written about as if they are real people. There is little awareness of Marlowe as the constructor of the text, and no links made to genre or other contexts. The writing style, while clear, lacks flair.

Sample answer 2

> To what extent do you agree that Marlowe presents Mephistopheles as nothing more than a deeply sinister and malevolent character?

These introductory sentences open up the possibility of debate by identifying some different ways of reading Mephistopheles's role.

As Lucifer's representative and the character who guides the protagonist to his tragic downfall, it is quite easy to see the sinister, malevolent qualities of Mephistopheles. His character in the play is varied, however: he is by turns a tempter, a companion, a sycophant and, in the end, a dangerous foil for Faustus. If the text were a straightforward morality play, then categorising Mephistopheles as a simply villainous character would be accurate but, in Doctor Faustus, Marlowe problematises the role of this character. At certain points in the narrative, we see a glimpse of a tormented character who possesses tragic potential.

Here the student adopts a suitable literary context, that of tragedy, and also acknowledges the playwright's hand in crafting the character.

Mephistopheles's first appearance in the play certainly suggests his sinister aspects, symbolically underscoring the danger he poses and his unearthly qualities. In performance, much is usually made of this dramatic moment to express his malevolence: the Greenwich production introduces a character whose demeanour provokes awe, if not fear, from both Faustus and the audience. The instruction from Faustus to 'return an old Franciscan friar' is obviously necessary for the character to have some corporeal presence on stage, but its deeper purpose is to symbolise that Mephistopheles is not what he appears.

A sense of the dramatic qualities of the play are touched on here, alongside a symbolic reading of his entrance. The student is making brisk, thoughtful points in this phase of the essay.

Marlowe makes us aware of Faustus's inability to see past the illusion of power that his newfound servant brings him. In Act II Scene I, as the Doctor wavers, the dramatic device of aside alerts the audience to Mephistopheles's true intent: he confides 'what will not I do to obtain his soul?' The irony in this situation is not lost on the audience, who see a supposedly intelligent man being manipulated. Yet this isn't comedy: Mephistopheles's intention is to win Faustus for Lucifer, so his manner is clearly sinister. As the Doctor flirts with salvation, Mephistopheles offers distraction, doing anything to bolster Lucifer's aims.

Yet from the first act, Marlowe gives lines to Mephistopheles that suggest his suffering. He observes his own torment – 'this is hell, nor am I out of it' – and urges Faustus not to follow the path he has set out upon. Something close to pity might be engendered here when he recounts the 'ten thousand hells' and the deprivation of heaven. However, the audience has to reconcile these moments with the actions of the character. One view may be that Mephistopheles is a version of a tragic character: his own actions contribute to his misery, his self-awareness allows him to witness his suffering and his actions mean a type of death – one of the soul. In this view of the character, Mephistopheles is more than a diabolical entity.

However, a less charitable view of this apparently tragic confession is that it is a ruse to manipulate Faustus. It certainly has the desired effect, because he provokes Faustus's bravado. Even if this hint of tragic suffering is taken at face value, it's overwhelmed by Mephistopheles's actions elsewhere. He dismisses the sacrament of marriage, steers Faustus from salvation, plays the sycophant and insults the Pope. There is a sense in which his friendship with Faustus, which grows in Acts 3 and 4, may endear him in part to the audience – often the events of these Acts are played as a comic double act – and yet it is always the case that his intentions are villainous. It is Mephistopheles who encourages Faustus's suicide in Act V Scene I by presenting him with a dagger; it is Mephistopheles who threatens to 'in piecemeal tear thy flesh'; it is Mephistopheles who physically tortures the Old Man.

For some readers, the character may provoke a fleeting thought that pity is possible, but maybe that is Marlowe's point: a failure to see the devil for what he is leads to disaster so, although Faustus is taken in, an astute reader of this play isn't. Mephistopheles is precisely as he appears to us – a sinister and malign representative of evil.

This paragraph contains a well-chosen example of the irony at work in the play and also some of the dramatic choices. There is a feeling that the student is handling the debate well and offering a view clearly.

Once more, well-selected examples help to bolster this counter-argument and the interesting idea that Mephistopheles may be seen in a tragic light is raised.

The fluency of the writing helps here. Includes the perceptive idea that the character has a symbolic death.

The argument is really convincing here. The student writes with confidence and several pertinent examples from the text are briskly interwoven to strengthen the case being made.

The final point is perceptive and makes an interesting distinction between Faustus's and the audience's perception. The argument is clinched in the final phase of the response with the task focus remaining secure throughout.

Taken together, this response is highly effective: it focuses on the task very closely and the argument feels convincing. References are used well and a good awareness of method is shown. The personal voice comes through in the writing, which is committed and fluently written. Links to the tragic genre are effective.

Writing about extracts

There will be times when you are required to write in detail about a scene or a section of the text, and so it is important that you are aware of the skills you need to practise if you write a close analysis of a specified part of the play.

Unlike a traditional essay, an extract task directs you to a specific moment in the play as the place to begin your answer. Yet it is essential that you look closely at the accompanying task because you are unlikely to be asked to write a running commentary on the extract. Instead, a debate or opinion is likely to be offered, and your job is to use the extract as a starting point to explore that debate or opinion. Extract tasks invariably require you to broaden out your answer to the rest of the play, and make links between the content of the extract and what happens elsewhere in the story.

When you are presented with an extract, you might ask the following questions before you begin to frame an answer.

- Identify where in the play does the extract comes from. What has happened in the previous scene? What happens in the next scene?
- What is happening in the extract? What is the plot outline?
- Which characters appear in the extract? Who has most lines? Are any characters on stage but silent?
- Where is the scene set? Is there anything to be said about stage directions?
- Is this a scene where action is important or is it a 'quiet' scene where the reflections of the characters are more important?
- How does the extract commence? Is there anything significant about the first line?
- How does the extract end? Is there anything significant about the last line?
- How is dialogue used? Is there a soliloquy?
- What major themes are explored in the extract?
- Does this extract introduce a new character or theme?
- Are earlier events echoed in the extract?
- Does the extract have any bearing on the end of the play?
- Does this extract change your mind about any of the characters?

Once you have made notes on the general direction and point of the extract, turn your attention to the task. As ever, identify the debate or opinion at the heart of the task. Here are some specific things you could do:

- Underline the key terms in the task and make concrete links between the terms and the content of the extract.
- Reread the extract, highlighting key pieces of dialogue or quotations that link with the task.

- Begin to frame your argument, making a list of clear points you would make in your answer.

- Consider the rest of the play and how it links to the extract in terms of character or theme. Select parts of the play or quotations that will illuminate your answer, or ones which might provide you with an alternative view.

- Work on your concluding point. What is your central argument/opinion?

There are no firm rules about how you arrange your response. You might start by looking closely at the extract and then move on to the remainder of the play. It is also possible to start with the rest of the play and then end by focusing on the extract. A third approach could be to move between the extract and other parts of the play at various points in your essay. However you choose to structure your writing, it is wise to spend roughly 50% of your time on the extract and 50% on the remainder of the play.

Activity 9

Use the following task to help you refine your ability to write about extracts.

> Explore the ways evil is presented in Act V Scene I. How far would you agree that, in the rest of the play, evil is shown as a powerful and frightening entity?

a) Read the task and extract carefully, and then plan an answer.

b) Once you have made a plan, draft an introduction and a conclusion.

Activity 10

Before you look at a sample response, look closely at your plan and identify your own strengths and areas for development. Use these prompts to help you:

- How closely have I focused on the debate/opinion set up in the task?

- What is the quality of my argument? How convincing and detailed are the points I intend to make?

- Have I explored the extract in detail? How well have I chosen quotations from the extract?

- What do I intend to say about method, context and genre?

- How much do I plan to say about other parts of the play?

- How fluent and effective is my introduction and conclusion?

Read the first half of the following sample response to the question, taking note of the points made.

Sample answer 3, first half

Explore the ways evil is presented in Act V Scene I. How far would you agree that in the rest of the play, evil is shown as a powerful and frightening entity?

Act V Scene I is part of the build-up towards the climactic following scene where Faustus is dragged to hell, and so, in presenting evil in Scene I, what we really see is how malevolent forces are gathering around the protagonist in preparation for his demise. Marlowe shows us that even at this late stage, the Doctor still doesn't appear fully aware of the way evil operates upon him.

The scene opens with Wagner's account of Faustus's actions. Initially, there is a quiet and sombre quality to Wagner's words, but he draws attention to the oddity of Faustus's feasting. What is particularly interesting in the first part of this scene is the silence of Mephistopheles: he stands by while the Scholars and Faustus engage in dialogue. One way of reading the dramatic choice here is to see it as symbolising the way in which evil operates – it insidiously and quietly goes about the business of corrupting souls undetected.

In this scene, evil is seen in actions as much as words. It is blindingly obvious to all on stage that Helen is merely an infernal conjuration. Here we see how evil works – it presents itself as virtue, all the while concealing its intent. Much like the ghost in *Hamlet*, which is feared to be the devil assuming 'a pleasing shape', Helen is precisely that. Evil is therefore shown to be deceptive: it is the innocent flower concealing the serpent. In performance, it is interesting to note how Mephistopheles reacts at this point: Helen is his conjuration and represents part of his attempt to damn Faustus, so the silent, deadly servant of Lucifer may well convey his barely concealed glee at this stage in his plan.

A much more disturbing moment of evil occurs midway through this scene when Faustus wavers after the Old Man's speech. At this point, sinister intent is no longer concealed, but direct and visible. Faustus's disturbing 'Hell calls for right' declaration as Mephistopheles hands Faustus a dagger reveals evil for what it is – a fatal pursuit of the soul. Evil is locked in a battle with good, a power struggle for control of humanity, and it pursues its case not with love but with threat and violence. Mephistopheles proclaims, 'I'll in piecemeal tear thy flesh'. Yet later in the scene, he returns to sycophantic wheedling when he assures Faustus that the Doctor's desire to see Helen shall be 'performed in the twinkling of an eye'.

Evil's ability to deceive is rendered dramatically when Faustus sexually interacts with the spirit of Helen. Ironically, the most beautiful poetry in the play is directed at the very thing that damns Faustus, a brilliantly ironic symbol of the power of evil. And yet the final words of the scene suggest that the power of evil is an illusion. The Old Man recognises that his faith 'shall triumph over thee' and so, in leaving the scene on this note, Marlowe reminds the reader of the power and also powerlessness of the malevolent forces in the world of the text.

Activity 12

The second part of the task in Activity 9 asks you to consider to what extent evil is shown as a powerful and frightening entity in the rest of the play.

Write the second half of this response, looking closely at how evil is presented in the remainder of the play and whether it can be accurately described as frightening.

Activity 13

Use the following task to help you practice your ability to write about extracts. Read the task and extract carefully, and then write an answer.

> Explore the ways Marlowe presents Faustus's power in Act IV Scene III. Consider whether Faustus is a powerful character in the rest of the play.

Writing answers

One of the most important elements of your response is phrasing. As well as taking time to select quotations and build an argument, you should also take time to work on your written expression. At the very least, you need to write with clarity, ensuring there are no vague sentences, or sections in which your point is obscured by inexact wording.

Reading widely is the best way to improve your phrasing. The more texts you access, the more sentence constructions and individual words you will encounter and adapt for your own purposes. Literary criticism has a certain style, so the more academic writing you read, including journals, study guides, critical magazines and essays, the more you will get a feel for the voice of literary criticism. Broaden your reading by accessing broadsheet newspapers online and reading novels slightly beyond your comfort zone. Listen to spoken radio programmes and engage in discussion with other students when possible. Above all, craft your writing. Draft and redraft your phrasing until it conveys precisely what you want it to say.

Sample questions

1

To what extent do you agree with the view that Faustus is a character who deserves his damnation?

2

Explore the view that it is more accurate to classify the play as a tragedy than as a morality play.

3

How far would you agree that the comic scenes in *Doctor Faustus* are the most memorable parts of the play?

4

Consider the role and function of Mephistopheles in the play. Is he impossible to sympathise with?

5

Explore the role of the Chorus in the Prologue. Is it accurate to say that the Chorus takes a disapproving view of Faustus in the play as a whole?

6

Explore the presentation of the Pope in Act III Scene I. How far is it true that religious figures are mocked in the rest of the play?

Glossary

allegory a story in which the characters have symbolic meaning

alliteration the repetition of consonant sounds at the start of words

anagnorisis a moment of recognition where the protagonist realises the significance of their mistake

archetype a model of a character type

aside a line delivered to the audience that cannot be heard by other characters

backstory events that have happened before the play begins

blank verse unrhymed lines of iambic pentameter

caesura a break or pause in a line of verse

catastrophe the climactic moment when disaster strikes

catharsis the emotional release felt by the audience, a sense of cleansing

character arc the 'journey' of a character during a story

Chorus a character(s) who offers comment on the action of the play to the audience

complication an event that intensifies an existing conflict

dialogue an exchange of lines between two or more characters

dramatic irony where the audience possess more knowledge than the character(s) on stage

dramatic tragedy a play showing the suffering and demise of the protagonist

elevated language words that rise above the ordinary, often in beautifully poetic ways

epithet an adjective or phrase thought to describe someone aptly and used to criticise or praise them

eponymous referring to a character whose name is also the title of the text

essentialist looking for the essence of a character itself, as though the character had a 'real' existence

farce a comic dramatic work including crude characterisation and ridiculously improbable situations

hamartia a mistake made by the protagonist, which leads to their downfall

hubris excessive pride, which leads characters to ignore warnings and presume that they know best

hyperbole deliberately exaggerated phrases

iambic pentameter a line of ten syllables consisting of five unstressed and five stressed syllables

imagery the use of visual or other sensual references

lyrical having an emotional and imaginative quality

magus a magician or sorcerer

metafictional referring to narratives that draw attention to their artifice; parts of stories that acknowledge their literary qualities

metaphor a figure of speech describing a person or thing by comparing them with something that is not literally applicable

modal verb a type of verb conveying intent or possibility, e.g. must, may, will, should, etc.

monosyllabic referring to words of one syllable

morality play a medieval play in which symbolic characters such as Virtue and Vice competed for the attention of the central character

muse a source of inspiration; in Greek mythology, the Muses were nine goddesses who presided over the arts and sciences

parody imitation of a person or thing for comic effect

peripeteia a catastrophe undergone by the protagonist; a reversal of fortune

polysemy the existence of more than one meaning for words

polysyllabic referring to words with several syllables

protagonist the central character; sometimes, but not always, a hero

representational seeing characters and situations as constructs – versions of 'real' characters and events. Representational readings place emphasis on how they have been shown by the author and what they reveal about the values of society and the author

resolution the part of a story where problems are resolved

rhetorical referring to speech or text intended to influence or persuade

satire humour used to make a serious point

soliloquy a speech made by an actor alone on stage, generally reflecting on thoughts and feelings

trochaic referring to a rhythm that inverts the iambic stress, i.e. a stressed syllable followed by an unstressed syllable

OXFORD
UNIVERSITY PRESS

Great Clarendon Street, Oxford, OX2 6DP, United Kingdom

Oxford University Press is a department of the University of Oxford. It furthers the University's objective of excellence in research, scholarship, and education by publishing worldwide. Oxford is a registered trade mark of Oxford University Press in the UK and in certain other countries

British Library Cataloguing in Publication Data

Data available

ISBN 978-019-843749-9

Kindle edition ISBN 978-019-843752-9

10 9 8 7 6 5 4 3 2 1

Printed in Hong Kong by Sheck Wah Tong Printing Press Ltd.

Acknowledgements

We are grateful for the permission to reprint the following copyright texts:

Excerpts from **The Holy Bible, New International Version®**, NIV® (Biblica Inc., 2011). Copyright © 1973, 1978, 1984, 2011 by Biblica, Inc.™ Reproduced with permission from Biblica, Inc. All rights reserved worldwide.

Excerpts from *Thucydides Mythhistoricus* (Edward Arnold Ltd., 1907). Reproduced with permission from Taylor & Francis Ltd. http://www.informaworld.com

A. Duxfield: *'Resolve me of all ambiguities'*: Doctor Faustus and the Failure to Unify, Early Modern Literary Studies Special Issue 16, pp.7.1-21 (EMLS, 2007). © 2007, Matthew Steggle (Editor, EMLS). Reproduced with permission from Early Modern Literary Studies.

A. Duxfield: *Review of Marlowe's Doctor Faustus at The Swan Theatre, Stratford-upon-Avon, 9 June 2016 and Jonson's The Alchemist at The Swan Theatre, Stratford-upon-Avon, 10 June 2016,* Shakespeare 13:1, pp.88-90 (Routledge, 2016). Reproduced with permission from Taylor & Francis Ltd. http://www.informaworld.com

W. Farnham: *Twentieth Century Interpretations of Doctor Faustus; a collection of critical essays.* pp.5 (Prentice-Hall, 1969). Reproduced with permission from Pearson Education, Inc., New York.

R. M. Frye: *Marlowe's Doctor Faustus: The Repudication of Humanity*, South Atlantic Quarterly 55:3, pp.322-328 (Duke University Press, 1956). Reproduced with permission from Duke University Press. www.dukeupress.edu

G. K. Hunter: *Five Act Structure in Doctor Faustus*, The Tulane Drama Review 8:4, pp.77-91 (The MIT Press, 1964) Reproduced with permission from MIT Press.

L. Kirschbaum: *Marlowe's Faustus: A Reconsideration*, Review of English Studies XIX, pp.229 (Oxford University Press, 1943). Reproduced with permission from Oxford University Press.

S. Orgel: as found in *Doctor Faustus*, edited by David Scott Kastan, Norton Critical Editions (WW Norton & Co, 2005). Reproduced with permission from Taylor & Francis Group Ltd.

R. B. Sewell: *The Vision of Tragedy* (Yale University Press, 1959) Reproduced with permission from Paragon House.

S. Snyder: *Marlowe's "Doctor Faustus" as an Inverted Saint's Life*, Studies in Philology 63:4, pp.565-577 (University of North Carolina Press, 1966), Reproduced with permission from North Carolina Press. www.uncpress.org

J. B. Steane: *Marlowe: A Critical Study* (Cambridge University Press, 1964). Reproduced with permission from Cambridge University Press.

W. J. Thoms: *Early English Prose Romances* (Nattali and Bond, 1858). Courtesy of Perseus Digital Library at Tufts University. Reproduced under the terms of the Creative Commons Attribution-ShareAlike 3.0 United States License.

C. Wiegand: *Your own personal demon: Maria Aberg on her Doctor Faustus double act*, Theatre, 12 February (The Guardian, 2016). Copyright Guardian News & Media Ltd 2019. Reproduced with permission from Guardian News & Media Ltd.

We have tried to trace and contact all copyright holders before publication. If notified, the publishers will be pleased to rectify any error or omissions at the earliest opportunity.

The publisher and authors would like to thank the following for permission to use photographs and other copyright material:

Cover: © Christophe Dessaigne/Trevillion Images. **p7:** The Picture Art Collection/Alamy Stock Photo; **p10:** © Photostage; **p16:** The Pepys Library, Magdalene College, Cambridge; **p19:** The History Collection/Alamy Stock Photo; **p24:** Science History Images/Alamy Stock Photo; **p29:** Ian Dagnall/Alamy Stock Photo; **p32:** The History Collection/Alamy Stock Photo; **p34:** Wellcome Collection/CC BY 4.0; **p35:** Pictorial Press Ltd/Alamy Stock Photo; **p36:** 360b/Alamy Stock Photo; **p39:** Granger Historical Picture Archive/Alamy Stock Photo; **p41:** Everett Collection Inc/Alamy Stock Photo; **p43:** INTERFOTO/Alamy Stock Photo; **p45:** Photostage; **p51:** Geraint Lewis/Alamy Stock Photo; **p57:** Jonathan Keenan; **p58:** dpa picture alliance archive/Alamy Stock Photo; **p62:** Marc Brenner; **p65:** Moviestore collection Ltd/Alamy Stock Photo; **p68:** classicpaintings/Alamy Stock Photo; **p72:** World History Archive/Alamy Stock Photo; **p74:** Photostage; **p78:** Keith Corrigan/Alamy Stock Photo; **p80:** ScreenProd/Photononstop/Alamy Stock Photo; **p83:** Photostage; **p85:** Keith Pattison/Shakespeare's Globe; **p87:** Photo by Helen Maybanks © RSC; **p91:** Photostage; **p93:** AF archive/Alamy Stock Photo; **p99:** From Chap-Books of the Eighteenth Century by Jogh Ashton, Chatto and Windus, Piccadilly , 1882/www.gutenberg.org; **p101:** Geraint Lewis/Alamy Stock Photo.

Every effort has been made to contact copyright holders of material reproduced in this book. Any omissions will be rectified in subsequent printings if notice is given to the publisher.